Matrimonial Finance Toolkit

CW01084230

Related titles from Law Society Publishing:

Children and Families Act 2014
Noel Arnold

Family Law Arbitration
Dennis Sheridan and Suzanne Kingston

Family Law Protocol (4th edn)
The Law Society

Good Practice in Child Care Cases (3rd edn)
The Law Society

Unbundling Family Legal Services Toolkit
Ursula Rice and Mena Ruparel

All books from Law Society Publishing can be ordered through good bookshops or direct from our distributors, Prolog, by telephone 0370 850 1422 or email **lawsociety@prolog.uk.com**. Please confirm the price before ordering.

For further information or a catalogue, please contact our editorial and marketing office by email **publishing@lawsociety.org.uk**.

Matrimonial Finance Toolkit

Mena Ruparel

The Law Society

ISBN 978-1-78446-090-7

Published in 2017 by the Law Society
113 Chancery Lane, London WC2A 1PL

Typeset by Columns Design XML Ltd, Reading
Printed by Hobbs the Printers Ltd, Totton, Hants

The paper used for the text pages of this book is FSC® certified. FSC (the Forest Stewardship Council®) is an international network to promote responsible management of the world's forests.

Contents

Preface   vii

Abbreviations   ix

1   First steps   1
       Annex 1A   Letter to client explaining applications that can be made for
                  financial remedy   5
       Annex 1B   Letter/paragraphs explaining pension options   9
       Annex 1C   Letter to client explaining the different processes that can be
                  used to resolve a financial remedy matter   12
       Annex 1D   Letter to client regarding change of circumstances   15
       Annex 1E   Letter to petitioner client regarding when to apply for the
                  Decree Absolute/Final Order   17
       Annex 1F   Letter to client to sever joint tenancy   19
       Annex 1G   Letter to client to explain home rights charge or restrictions 20

2   Making a financial remedy application   22
       Annex 2A   Completed extract from Form A   28
       Annex 2B   Letter to mortgage company sending sealed Form A   33
       Annex 2C   Letter to pension trustees sending sealed Form A   34
       Annex 2D   Letter to a third party advising them about financial remedy
                  proceedings   35

3   Disclosure   36
       Annex 3A   Letter explaining information required for voluntary
                  disclosure   59
       Annex 3B   Letter explaining to the client the documents required for
                  Form E   62
       Annex 3C   Letter to client explaining disclosure requirements, self-help
                  and online protection   64
       Annex 3D   Schedule of expenditure of applicant/respondent   66
       Annex 3E   Letter enclosing Form E to the other side and the court 69
       Annex 3F   Letter enclosing other party's Form E and next steps   70
       Annex 3G   Statement of issues   72
       Annex 3H   Request for further information and documents – 'the
                  questionnaire'   73
       Annex 3I   Chronology   74
       Annex 3J   Schedule of assets   75

4   First directions appointment   78
       Annex 4A   Letter to the client before the first appointment   84
       Annex 4B   Letter to the client enclosing the FDA order   86
       Annex 4C   Letter instructing a property expert   88
       Annex 4D   Letter to pension valuer   92

Annex 4E Letter to SJE forensic/business accountant   96
Annex 4F Letter to SJE accountant to obtain CGT calculations   100
Annex 4G Letter to the client enclosing the expert's report   103

5   **Financial dispute resolution**   **104**
Annex 5A Without prejudice letter to settle   110
Annex 5B Letter to the other side advising on the without prejudice
          offer   113
Annex 5C Letter to the client before the financial dispute resolution
          hearing   116

6   **Final hearing**   **119**
Annex 6A Trial bundle index   123
Annex 6B Letter to the client sending the FDR order   125
Annex 6C Outline section 25 statement   127
Annex 6D Open position   129

7   **Draft orders**   **132**
Annex 7A FDA order   138
Annex 7B FDR order   142
Annex 7C Consent order   145

8   **Schedule 1 Children Act proceedings**   **148**
Annex 8A First letter to applicant in Schedule 1 Children Act claim 154
Annex 8B Draft order Schedule 1   157

Preface

When I qualified as a solicitor I used a book similar to this to get me through the drafting issues that faced me daily. The Form E was introduced about a year after I qualified and all practitioners had to get to grips with the intricacies of the form and the preparation of the new questionnaire and statement of issues. It was a very different way of working as previously we had been drafting freehand, which is now almost unheard of. The way that these documents are drafted today is quite different from the way that they were drafted then.

It is my hope that practitioners will find this toolkit useful as it contains many practical precedents to get matrimonial practitioners through the week without tearing their hair out. Even experienced practitioners are plagued by preparing letters of instruction to single joint experts and so I have provided four precedents that should cover every base.

I would like to thank a number of fellow practitioners for their assistance in checking that these precedents are fit for purpose. Lewis Hulatt of Major Family Law has been a great help in going through the precedents and suggesting helpful amendments. Thanks also to Roopa Ahluwalia of Birketts solicitors, Karen Dovaston of Jefferies solicitors and Melanie Barnes of Major Family Law for their input.

Mark Penston of Bluesky chartered financial planners has helped with the tricky pensions sections of the Form E, the section on how to explain pensions to a client and the drafting of the single joint expert's letter at Annex 4D. Mark has been my 'go to' person for expertise on pensions for 10 years and I am grateful to him for his continued assistance.

I am aware that there are more practitioners than ever before moving into the field of matrimonial finance from other areas of law which are no longer financially viable. I hope that this toolkit will become a useful staple for their flourishing practices.

Mena Ruparel
July 2017

Abbreviations

CE	cash equivalent
CEv	cash equivalent valuation
CGT	Capital Gains Tax
CMS	Child Maintenance Service
CPI	Consumer Price Index
FDA	first directions appointment
FDR	financial dispute resolution
FPR 2010	Family Procedure Rules 2010, SI 2010/2955
FRWG	Financial Remedies Working Group
IFA	independent financial adviser
MCA 1973	Matrimonial Causes Act 1973
MIAM	mediation information and assessment meeting
PPF	Pension Protection Fund
PRPA	person responsible for the pension arrangement
SJE	single joint expert
SRA	Solicitors Regulation Authority

1 First steps

1.1 Introduction

It is anticipated that after a practitioner initially sees a client, the practitioner will follow up by writing to the client with an initial letter of advice, the firm's client care letter and the firm's terms and conditions of business (if these have not already been sent).

Thereafter, clients will need some information about non-court dispute resolution processes, the applications that they can make and the processes they will be expected to go through. The precedent letters in this chapter provide guidance for the practitioner to deliver this information to the client, in a way that is both comprehensive and easy to understand.

The practitioner may wish to adapt these letters, depending on the information already given. It is envisaged that these letters will be sent before litigation proceedings have commenced. There are a number of different ways that the practitioner can address the client, but these letters assume that clients are referred to by their preferred forename. Likewise, when the spouse is referred to, their forename is used. The parties could be referred to as 'Mr and Mrs' (or an appropriate alternative), but that is a more formal approach.

These precedents are for use in divorce or dissolution cases. It will be noted that where the terminology in civil partnership cases is slightly different from that in divorce, the precedents provide for both alternatives. In these notes where the Decree Absolute is referenced, the reader should assume that the final decree in dissolution proceedings is also being referred to.

1.2 Explaining the financial remedy process to the client

The letter at **Annex 1A** sets out the various financial remedy applications that can be made by the client. It explains when those applications can be made at court, as clients are often surprised that these claims survive the pronouncement of the Decree Absolute. It is important that the client understands that the claims themselves arise as a result of the marriage and that the pronouncement of the Decree Absolute does not bring those claims to an end. If there are no children of the family then the paragraphs relating to maintenance orders for children should be deleted.

Whilst there is not too much detail in this initial letter about pensions, **Annex 1B** contains additional paragraphs that can be added to **Annex 1A** if necessary.

Annex 1B can be utilised after mediation has taken place as the parties will both aware of each other's pension valuations at that stage. There is a fine balance to be struck between giving clients enough information and overwhelming them with too much information.

As soon as you become aware that your client's spouse has a pension, it is sensible to write to your client and set out the post-divorce pension options. In some cases (especially during mediation or amicable separations), seeking advice from a suitably qualified independent financial adviser can be helpful in providing thoughts on how pension sharing should be approached and whether any actions prior to pension sharing would be advantageous to both parties.

Some suitably qualified independent financial advisers can produce pension sharing reports and associated relevant advice. Actuaries are not regulated by the Financial Conduct Authority (FCA) and although they can produce pension sharing reports, they are unable to provide financial advice to your clients.

These paragraphs can also be adapted to ensure that if clients have a significant pension, they are aware that their spouses could make these claims against the pension.

These paragraphs can be inserted into a letter after the client attends mediation and has information about the spouse's pension. It can be used in the litigation process after Forms E are exchanged as the pension information should be known at that point.

It is important that the client understands that solicitors are not authorised to give financial advice. The letter specifies that this is an offence under the Financial Services and Markets Act 2000. Many clients do not want to pay for an expert to get involved or to see a financial adviser about this issue. It is important that they understand at an early stage that the solicitor can only give general advice about pension options. Any specific advice needs to be obtained from an independent financial adviser (IFA) or Chartered Financial Planner.

The Solicitors Regulation Authority (SRA) Code of Conduct 2011 sets out that if a solicitor wants to refer a third party to a client, the recommendation must be in the best interests of the client. Any financial or business interest in making the referral needs to be disclosed to the client, and the solicitor should not be paid a prohibited referral fee. There is nothing in the Code that says that only an *independent* financial adviser is referred, only that the client must be in a position to make an informed decision about how to pursue their matter (Outcome 6.3). The Law Society believes that the SRA provision is too widely drawn and that the profession should only refer to IFAs ('Law Society warning over new SRA financial adviser rule', Law Society press release, 29 November 2012).

If the client refuses to take any financial advice about pensions, the solicitor should consider whether it is possible to safely proceed to negotiate a settlement. As a minimum, a waiver should be signed by clients to confirm that they have been strongly advised to take independent financial advice and they have chosen not to do so. Ideally, the waiver should be witnessed by two people and the original should be kept in a safe place with the file.

When issuing file closing instructions, consideration should be given to keeping the file for six years after the date when the pension will be drawn by the client, just in case a negligence claim is made.

1.3 Explaining the non-court dispute remedy choices to the client

The letter at **Annex 1C** sets out the importance of non-court dispute resolution. It also refers to best practice guidance from Resolution and the Law Society's Family Law Protocol. Whilst not all practitioners subscribe to the best practice provisions, it is important to note that they are widely used by specialist family law practitioners. Clients often seek out practitioners who follow these guidelines.

1.4 Circumstances in which early advice might change

In certain circumstances the practitioner may have been able to give clients advice at an early stage. This is more likely if they have been to mediation and have completed disclosure with their spouse. The letter at **Annex 1D** deals with the issue that any initial advice is subject to change. Most practitioners do not give advice until they have seen all of the evidence. After mediation, the parties may be happy with the disclosure given even if no documentation has been exchanged between the parties. It may later transpire that the evidence does not support the disclosure given at mediation. If this is the case, then any initial advice given to the client will change and this letter makes that clear.

In the event that the parties have not been able to reach an agreement at mediation, the client may seek advice at that stage whether to pursue further negotiations or to issue proceedings.

Clients are often unaware of the length of time the litigation process can take and the inherent delays within proceedings. The client should be told at an early stage that initial advice given about settlement prospects may be superseded if circumstances change. For example, if the client has savings of £50,000, the client should be made aware that these funds may erode during the course of proceedings. The value of underlying investments may change, increasing or decreasing in value over time.

Clients should also be made aware that if significant judgments are handed down by the higher courts during the course of the proceedings, any advice given at an early stage will change. The letter at **Annex 1D** is not intended to unsettle clients but, rather, is intended to ensure that they realise that the landscape of their finances is in a constant state of flux.

1.5 The effect of applying for the Decree Absolute on financial remedy claims

At an early stage in the divorce proceedings the client needs to know that important benefits can be lost when the Decree Absolute is pronounced. As stated above, they do not lose the right to make financial remedy claims after the pronouncement of the Decree Absolute. Ideally, the practitioner will have taken this into account very early on in the divorce process. If pension benefits are likely to be lost, the petitioner should have asked the respondent to give an undertaking not to apply for the Decree Absolute until financial matters have been resolved by way of court order. Such an undertaking is not always forthcoming and those issues straddle divorce and financial matters. **Annex 1E** can be adapted so that the core information from para.3 onwards can be inserted into standard letters in divorce proceedings.

1.6 The importance of property in financial remedy cases

Annex 1F is a letter dealing with the ownership of any property (or properties) that vests jointly in the client and their spouse. Once that information is obtained by getting copies of the Land Registry entries, the client will need advice about the possible severance of the joint tenancy. **Annex 1G** is a letter dealing with the issue of a property (or properties) owned by one party in their sole name. It should be remembered that the home rights notice (registered using Form HR1 at the Land Registry for registered land) only protects the right of the non-owner to occupy. If the client has a financial interest in the land, the client should also register a restriction at the Land Registry using Form RX1. The Land Registry produces useful guides to explain these processes: 'Practice guide 19: notices, restrictions and the protection of third party interests in the register' and 'Practice guide 20: applications under the Family Law Act 1996' (otherwise known as 'home rights'). Both guides can be found at **www.gov.uk/government/publications**.

Annex 1A

Letter to client explaining applications that can be made for financial remedy

Dear [*name of client*]

Thank you for coming to see me with regard to the breakdown of your [marriage/ civil partnership]. Because of your [marriage/civil partnership] you can make financial claims against [*name of spouse/civil partner*].

If you want to make a financial claim, this can be done at the same time as your [divorce/dissolution] and at any time after the [Decree Absolute/Final Decree]. You can still make the court applications until you [remarry/enter into a civil partnership]. If these claims were noted by you in the divorce petition then you could even make the applications to court after remarriage.

It is advisable to make and finalise any financial claims that you have against [*name of spouse/civil partner*] now rather than wait until later. The longer you wait to pursue claims the more likely it is that complications will arise. This can happen, for example, when property values rise or fall, or when either of you buy new assets or receive an inheritance that you did not have during your [marriage/civil partnership]. Even if you win the lottery after the [divorce/dissolution] this can affect the financial distribution.

[I have written to you separately about using non-court dispute resolution. If you and [*name of spouse*] have decided to go to mediation, use collaborative law or use arbitration then you do not need to make financial claims at court straight away. Hopefully, you will be able to come to an agreement about your financial matters; if that is the case, then you will not need to make an application for the court to resolve matters. You will, however, need to turn the agreement into a draft consent order which is sent to the court to confirm the terms of settlement. The judge will decide if the terms are fair and the judge has a discretion to accept or reject the terms of the settlement. This is not a 'rubber stamp' exercise. The judge will need brief financial information about you both and will consider the agreement carefully.]

You can make the following claims against [*name of spouse*] in respect of your assets.

Property claims

It is possible for you to make a claim against any property that you own jointly with [*name of spouse*] or that [*name of spouse*] owns solely in [his/her] name. A claim against property can be a claim against land, residential property or even commercial property owned by [*name of spouse*].

The court can make an order to sell or transfer property either in England and Wales or abroad, or to change the terms on which it is owned and when any equity can be realised.

The court can also make orders transferring shares, life policies, contents of your property or collector's items.

[Any property owned by a trust or a limited company is beyond the direct reach of the court. As such the court cannot make orders to sell or transfer such property.]

Capital orders

The court can make lump sum orders for either you or [name of spouse] to pay the other a sum of money. This could be a one-off payment or a series of payments over a period of time. The structure of the payment will depend on the circumstances of the case.

The payment can be ordered to be made on a specified date or at the same time as the transfer or sale of a property.

Income orders

The court has the power to make various income orders for either your benefit, or [name of spouse]'s benefit. Payments can also be made to the child(ren) of the family.

Payments that are made between you and [name of spouse] are known as 'periodical payments' orders. One of you could be made to pay the other a regular monthly sum of money for a specified period of time or until the occurrence of a specific event.

The circumstances and length of the order depend very much upon the ages of any children, the amount that each of you can be expected to earn and the overall circumstances of the case. An order will be made if one party needs money (e.g. to pay the bills and housing costs) and the other party has surplus income (after bills and housing costs have been paid) from which 'periodical payments' can be made.

The court cannot make an order for one party to pay the other periodical payments once the receiving party remarries. It is mandatory that periodical payments end upon remarriage.

Financial support now

In some circumstances, the court can make an urgent order for one party to pay the other party maintenance whilst the proceedings for divorce/civil partnership are ongoing. As an interim measure, maintenance is usually paid at a lower rate than it might be in the long term. Interim maintenance is meant to cover the basic essentials, excluding long-term and capital expenses.

As set out above, the court will only make such an order in circumstances where the paying party has sufficient surplus income from which to pay maintenance and the receiving party has a shortfall of income and cannot pay their bills and other outgoings.

Legal services payment orders

It is possible to make an application to the court for [*name of spouse*] to pay your legal costs upfront if you are unable to find a way to pay for these costs yourself. This can be an expensive application to make and we should discuss this option, together with other funding options if you are unable to pay for your legal costs by using your own resources.

Maintenance orders for children

The Child Maintenance Service (CMS) generally deals with maintenance for children. The CMS website contains a wealth of information and I recommend that you look at it. There is an online calculator at **www.gov.uk/calculate-your-child-maintenance** that will help you and [*name of spouse*] to calculate the minimum sum of maintenance that should be paid.

There are limited circumstances in which the court will make an order for payments specifically for children.

Most commonly this will happen where you and [*name of spouse*] agree a sum of money that one of you will pay to the other for the benefit of the child(ren). This type of order by agreement is only binding upon both parties for the period of 12 months from the date of the order. After that period of time, either party can go to the CMS and make an application for a CMS calculation.

The court also has the ability to make orders in respect of children in the following additional circumstances:

(a) where the child(ren) suffer(s) from a disability;
(b) where the child(ren) [is/are] in full-time education or training;
(c) where the paying parent has been assessed to pay the maximum sum by the CMS, the court has the jurisdiction to make a 'top up' order;
(d) where either parent or the child resides overseas.

It is possible that the maintenance can extend beyond a child's 18th birthday and beyond the time a child is at university, in certain circumstances. It is important to note that the financial obligations you each have for your children cannot be terminated, unlike the financial obligations you and your spouse/civil partner may have towards each other.

Pension orders

The court can make the following types of pension order:

(a) pension attachment;
(b) pension sharing.

[Where pensions are being administered by the Pension Protection Fund the court can make the above orders against the Pension Protection Fund rather than the trustees of the pension. These are known as compensation orders.]

Pension orders are fairly complex and it may be that an expert's report is required in order to help you to decide how to structure a settlement. I will advise you when we need an expert's report. Please do not commission an expert's report yourself as this is usually done in a specific way to ensure that it can be used in court proceedings.

As soon as I know more about the pensions in your case I will advise you further.

Costs orders

It is very rare in family finance proceedings for the court to make a costs order. The general rule that the court will follow is that each party will pay their own legal costs.

In rare circumstances, the court will make a costs order against your [spouse/civil partner]. The court will usually do so in the following circumstances:

a) where one party has failed to comply with orders of the court, rules or practice directions;
b) where one party has pursued their case unreasonably;
c) where a party has defended their case unreasonably;
d) where one party made a reasonable open offer that should have been accepted but the other party did not accept it and thereby incurred further costs.

The court will only make orders where it is just and reasonable in all of the circumstances to do so and where it would not destabilise the final division of assets to make a costs order.

I would estimate that costs orders are made in less than 0.05% of cases. You should therefore be ready to fund your own litigation proceedings. There is little chance for the recovery of your legal costs unless [name of spouse] does something that the court considers sufficiently serious to justify departing from the general rule. This is because each of you is paying your costs out of family money.

I hope you understand the orders that the court is able to make. If you have any questions or queries please do not hesitate to contact me.

Yours sincerely

Annex 1B

Letter/paragraphs explaining pension options

I note that your spouse has a pension(s) that you might eventually share in some way. Pensions are a complex subject area and you might not be clear how to proceed in respect of this asset.

Please note that pensions are specialist, tax efficient investment vehicles that are designed to produce an income when you retire. The valuations provided are sometimes a poor reflection of the benefits that the scheme will provide and some schemes have valuable benefits that would be lost on transfer.

I would strongly recommend that you take independent financial advice from an adviser who is experienced in pensions and divorce matters at an early stage in respect of [*name of spouse*]'s pension(s) and the overall financial settlement. A number of financial advisers are accredited through an organisation called Resolution and any one of them will definitely be able to assist you.

There are a number of choices that you will eventually need to make about the pension(s). Note that although I will give you legal advice, I cannot provide you with financial advice, so you should also take independent financial advice.

If you do not have a financial adviser I can recommend the following independent financial advisers with whom I have worked in the past and who understand the importance of pensions within the divorce process.

1.
2.
3.

Please note that I am not authorised to give financial advice as this would be an offence under the Financial Services and Markets Act 2000.

[*Name of spouse*] has pension(s) and in respect of each pension you can take a share of the pension, attach it or offset your interest in the pension against other assets.

Pensions are complex assets and the value of a pension fund and the income it produces on retirement are two distinct matters.

Pension sharing

The court can make an order that [*name of spouse*]'s pension(s) are shared with you. You can either agree between you what percentage of the pension you will share, or the court will decide whether to make a pension sharing order. Normally, all pensions including the state pension are taken into account when calculating an appropriate percentage share. Sometimes the court can decide to exclude pensions that were built up before the date of the marriage. The court has the discretion to do this and may use it in appropriate cases.

In general, the person with the larger pension(s) will share some of their pension(s) with the person who has less by way of pension benefits.

In some cases, the pension trustees will allow you to become a separate member of the same scheme as your ex-spouse. They may insist on an external transfer of your pension share to a personal pension of your choice. As the choices can be complex, independent financial advice should be sought to establish which route is the best for you.

Only an independent financial adviser will be able to give you advice about what to do with your pension share once you get it. My role is to ensure that you get a fair share of assets, and once I have done that the financial adviser will tell you where to invest your pension.

Once pension sharing has been put into effect by the trustees of [*name of spouse*]'s pension, you will have your own pension fund.

Once you receive a share of [*name of spouse*]'s pension, this becomes your pension. It can't be taken away from you and it can't be varied. If [*name of spouse*] dies 28 days or more after you get a pension sharing order, your entitlement to get this pension is not affected by [his/her] death. You decide when you want to take your pension, subject to the rules of the pension scheme.

Pension attachment

This is another option for taking an interest in [*name of spouse*]'s pension. This option is rarely used these days as it does not create a 'clean break', which many individuals prefer. If you choose pension attachment you become entitled to a proportion of your ex-partner's pension, but have no influence over when or how your ex-partner takes benefits.

This can cause problems if [*name of spouse*] decides not to take the income from this pension until the age of 75, for example. The court has no power to order [*name of spouse*] to retire on a certain date or at a specific age. If [*name of spouse*] dies, then your entitlement to [his/her] pension income will stop. If you remarry, you will lose your pension income under the terms of this order.

Although the court will set out your entitlement to [*name of spouse*]'s pension in an order, this will always be subject to the possibility that [*name of spouse*] will apply for a variation of the order in the future. This means that the pension attachment order is not fixed but is subject to change.

After a pension attachment order has been made, [*name of spouse*] could stop making any contribution to this pension. You are not permitted to make a contribution to the pension as it remains in [*name of spouse*]'s name. This means that the pension may not increase in value at all between now and when [*name of spouse*] takes the pension income. You can of course start a pension in your sole name which is a matter you should discuss with your financial adviser.

Overall, most people find that pension attachment offers little certainty and so would not choose this option, although in rare cases there are valid reasons for considering it.

Pension offsetting

This is a way to take other assets instead of touching [*name of spouse*]'s pension(s). The difficulty is that there is no widely accepted way of calculating what is a fair sum to take instead of sharing the pension. The higher courts have stated that £1 in a pension fund is not worth £1 in savings, but we do not know any more than that.

Often, a pension's actuary/independent financial adviser or Chartered Financial Planner can be involved as a joint expert. This means that the expert is asked to provide a report to the court about pension distribution between you. The expert can be asked to calculate how much your share in [*name of spouse*]'s pension should be worth as an offsetting figure. The expert is likely to use two or three different methods of calculation as examples, rather than producing one final answer. This can be a useful aid to settlement or to a judge when deciding how the assets should be shared between you.

Annex 1C

Letter to client explaining the different processes that can be used to resolve a financial remedy matter

Dear [*name of client*]

Many thanks for coming to see me with regard to your matrimonial issues. I write to outline a number of dispute resolution processes that are available to you. These processes are voluntary and would require [*name of spouse*] to agree before you can proceed to use any of them.

As you know, I am a [Resolution member/Resolution accredited specialist/Member of the Family Law Accreditation at the Law Society/Member of the Family Law Advanced Accreditation at the Law Society]. This means that I am bound by the [Resolution code of conduct] as well as the [Law Society Family Law Protocol]. I am therefore committed to ensuring that I minimise any potential conflict within your relationship breakdown, as much as I am able to do so.

Many people think that they should have their 'day in court', which will lead to a final resolution of the dispute. In reality, this is not how modern disputes are usually resolved. The vast majority of people are able to reach a negotiated settlement without ever needing to issue a court application.

With that in mind I have outlined below various low-conflict options that you may choose to take advantage of to try to resolve any children or financial matters between you and [*name of spouse*]. There are many financial and other advantages that support using one or more of the options below.

Mediation

Mediation is a dispute resolution process that works very well for many couples. Many people confuse the process of mediation with that of reconciliation. The purpose of mediation is to support you to make decisions when you decide that your relationship has ended. Reconciliation is the process that you would go through if you want to get back together with [*name of spouse*].

The mediator is a neutral person who can help you and [*name of spouse*] to make decisions. I am happy to recommend a mediator to you who will be able to assist you through any conflict areas. Mediation is one of the most cost-effective and time-effective ways to resolve disputes. Mediators tend to have an average of three to six meetings with a couple to help you to resolve both children and financial matters.

Legal aid is still available to help fund the process of mediation and it may be that this is available to either you or [*name of spouse*]. If this is not an option, the precise cost is difficult to estimate, but I would expect the cost to be between £500 and £1,000.

Each mediator charges a different hourly rate and so you will need to find out the specific costs from the mediator when you are referred. I would recommend that you look at the video available at **www.gov.uk/government/publications/family-mediation,** as it will give you a good idea what mediation is and what mediators do.

If you are not able to reach an agreement during the mediation process, an outcome cannot be imposed on you.

Collaborative law

Collaborative law is a process whereby both parties engage solicitors who are specialists and who are trained in the collaborative law process.

This can be a low-conflict process and result in agreed settlements much more quickly than via litigation. The parties and their solicitors commit to the process of negotiation to avoid litigation. The solicitor's commitment is such that if the process does not result in an agreement, the solicitor will not be able to represent you in the litigation process. [I am trained in the collaborative law process] *or* [I am happy to refer you to a collaboratively trained solicitor] *or* [*Name of solicitor*] in our practice is collaboratively trained].

The cost of the collaborative law process is variable, as this usually depends on the hourly rate of each solicitor involved. It is likely to cost in the region of £2,000–£5,000 plus VAT.

If you are not able to reach an agreement during the collaborative law process, an outcome cannot be imposed on you.

Arbitration

Arbitration more closely resembles the court process because the arbitrator can make a decision if you and [*name of spouse*] do not reach an agreement first. The arbitrator can deal with most financial cases and in your case there does not seem to be any reason why you should not be able to use arbitration. If you are interested in using this process, please have a look at the leaflet prepared by the Institute of Family Arbitrators, available at **ifla.org.uk/divi/wp-content/uploads/Public.pdf.**

An independent arbitrator will be chosen by you and [*name of spouse*] who ensures that the evidence is collected and that each party has the opportunity to 'have their say'. The arbitrator then uses the information to make a decision about the division of assets, income, pensions and property between the parties. The decision of an arbitrator is called the arbitration 'award'.

Consent order

In each of the above processes, if a settlement is reached, a draft consent order will need to be prepared and sent to the Family Court. A judge has the power to accept or reject the terms of settlement that you reach between you at mediation or using the collaborative process.

If the consent order reflects the terms of an arbitrator's award it will not be rejected unless there are exceptional reasons to do so.

To many people it seems strange that a judge can refuse to accept the terms of an agreement that you have both reached between you. If the terms of the agreement are fair the judge won't interfere with the terms of the settlement. Sometimes the judge wants to know more about the settlement between the parties and asks questions before the terms of the draft order are approved.

On other occasions the judge will have some concerns about the way the document is drafted, and this will result in the order being re-drafted. The precedents that we will use to draft the consent order have been approved by the President of the Family Division so I can see no reason why this should happen. However, all judges have an absolute right to raise any questions that they want to.

Very rarely the judge will reject the terms of the settlement if they are deemed to be too favourable to one party. In this situation we will need to sit down and discuss the options going forward in your case.

Overall, the costs for drafting a consent order will be between £750 plus VAT and £2,000 plus VAT depending on how complicated the order is and whether the judge raises questions about the terms.

Please let me know if you would like any more information about any of the above processes so that you can decide how to progress matters forward.

Yours sincerely

Annex 1D

Letter to client regarding change of circumstances

Dear [*name of client*]

Many thanks for your instructions in this matter. I write to advise you that whilst I have given you my initial views on the settlement options, it is possible that these views might change.

Possible future changes of advice

I appreciate that this is a difficult time for you and your family and that you would like to make decisions based on the best advice. Unfortunately, the progress of litigation can be quite slow and this means that as your assets change and your personal circumstances change my advice may also need to change.

Legal costs

As a general rule of thumb, both parties will spend roughly equal sums on legal costs and these funds will therefore not be available to distribute. I refer you back to my initial estimate of costs in this matter. It can take 12 months or more to reach a final financial order, either by agreement or by order of the court. The money and property available to distribute at the end of the case can be quite different from that available at the beginning of the case.

The influence of higher courts

You should also be aware that the courts can sometimes change their attitudes towards certain outcomes. This can happen when a case is resolved by the Supreme Court or the Court of Appeal which impacts on similar cases ongoing in the Family Court across the country. I will try to ensure that you are made aware of any cases similar to yours that might be dealt with in the higher courts. To the best of my knowledge, there are no such cases at the moment. As family law specialists, we do everything we can to ensure that we keep you informed of such changes as and when they occur. Please rest assured that these changes happen infrequently.

Evidence changes

As time goes on in the litigation process, we will collect evidence from you and your spouse to send to court. Occasionally, my advice will change as a result of evidence produced which may impact on the case as I thought it was when I initially gave you advice.

Financial division

As I have already explained to you, there is no formula that guides the distribution of assets in divorce proceedings. This means that I can only advise you by using my knowledge of the way in which the Family Court in [*location*] deals with these matters in cases similar to yours.

I will do the best that I can to minimise any unnecessary changes of advice. You can help me by ensuring that I have your evidence when I ask you to provide it to me. You should also inform me of any change in circumstances as soon as they happen.

Yours sincerely

Annex 1E

Letter to petitioner client regarding when to apply for the Decree Absolute/Final Order

Dear [*name of client*]

I write to enclose the Decree Nisi certificate [Conditional Order] which was pronounced on [*date*] at the [*insert details of the Family Court*]. Please keep this document in a safe place as you may need to refer to it in the future.

When you can apply for the Decree Absolute

As you are the petitioner in the divorce, you are entitled to apply for the Decree Absolute/Final Order six weeks and one day after the date of the Decree Nisi/Conditional Order. Therefore, the first date that you can apply for the Decree Absolute/Final Order is [*date*].

Delay the application for Decree Absolute

We usually recommend that you do not apply for the Decree Absolute/Final Order until the financial matters have been resolved by way of a final financial remedy order. This is very important and there are very good reasons not to make the application.

If your spouse has a pension, you will currently benefit from a widow's/widower's pension in the event that your spouse dies before the Decree Absolute/Final Order is pronounced.

When the Decree Absolute/Final Order is pronounced, you will no longer be married to each other and you will not benefit from any widow's/widower's pension if your spouse dies before we get a final order. It is possible that you will receive a pension sharing order as part of the overall financial settlement. It is sensible to wait for the final financial order to be made before you apply for the Decree Absolute/Final Order, so that your right to your spouse's death benefit is protected.

You might think that it is in your interests to apply for the Decree Absolute/Final Order at the first opportunity. If you think that you want to apply as soon as you can, we should discuss this.

When can [*name of spouse*] apply for the Decree Absolute/Final Order?

Eventually, [*name of spouse*] can apply for the Decree Absolute/Final Order in their own right. The first date that [he/she] may do so is 3 months after the first date that you can apply. Therefore, I calculate that [*name of spouse*] will be able to apply for the Decree Absolute/Final Order on [*date*].

Can we stop [*name of spouse*] from applying for the Decree Absolute/Final Order?

We may be able to prevent [*name of spouse*] from applying for the Decree Absolute/Final Order by asking them to give us an undertaking not to apply for the Decree Absolute/Final Order until the final financial order is made. An undertaking is a solemn promise not to do something; however, [*name of spouse*] is not obliged to give us that promise.

If [*name of spouse*] does not give that promise, you should be aware that recent case law suggests that [*name of spouse*] will be able to obtain the Decree Absolute/Final Order unless there are exceptional circumstances that prevent it from being granted. Your case does not exhibit the necessary exceptional circumstances. In my view, we would be unlikely to persuade a court to prevent your spouse from obtaining the Decree Absolute/Final Order. We can discuss this possibility at the point at which you can apply for the Decree Absolute/Final Order as we should know more about the financial settlement by then.

[*To be used in cases where there is a home rights notice:* As your spouse owns the former matrimonial home in [his/her] sole name we have registered your right to occupy the property. If you apply for the Decree Absolute/Final Order to be granted then you will no longer be married to each other and your right to occupy the property will terminate. Your spouse will be able to cancel the home rights notice by submitting the Decree Absolute/Final Order to the Land Registry. We may be able to make an application to extend your right to occupy the property.]

Wills

You should also be aware that whilst you remain married your existing wills continue to take effect against each other. Once the Decree Absolute/Final Order is pronounced you will both need to make new wills.

Should you wish to discuss this any further please do not hesitate to contact me.

Yours sincerely

Annex 1F

Letter to client to sever joint tenancy

Dear [*name of client*]

I am writing to you further to our meeting as I have now obtained the necessary information from the Land Registry in respect of your property.

It is clear to me now that you and [*name of co-owner*] own the property at [*address(es) of property*] as Joint Tenants. This means that you own the property as a whole between you and that in the event either of you dies, the other will automatically own the whole property. This is known as the right of survivorship.

It is possible to change the way that you own the property by doing what is known as 'severing the joint tenancy'. This is done by preparing a legal document and sending it to [*name of spouse*]. If you want to do this, then you and [*name of spouse*] will still be joint owners but you will own the property as Tenants in Common. This will mean that you will each own 50% of the property and you will each be able to leave your share by will to whoever you wish.

It is not possible to sever the tenancy in unequal shares. Choosing to sever the tenancy now will not jeopardise your claim in financial proceedings to a greater share of the equity in this property. It will not limit the way in which the Court can deal with the property in the financial case.

This is an interim measure designed to allow you flexibility to leave your share of the property on death to whoever you choose.

It is your choice whether you decide to sever the tenancy or not. You should be aware that once the tenancy is severed, [*name of spouse*]'s share will not pass to you automatically in the event of their death.

Please can you let me know in writing whether you wish to sever the joint tenancy. You can do this by signing the enclosed copy of this letter and sending it to me. I will then prepare the necessary paperwork to send to [*name of co-owner*].

It is vital that you make a will at the same time as severing the joint tenancy. This is so that you leave your share to your chosen beneficiaries.

If you choose to go ahead, then once the tenancy has been severed I will register this change at the Land Registry.

Yours sincerely

[*Insert signature clause on a duplicate copy of the letter*]

I confirm that I do/not want you to go ahead and sever the tenancy for the above property.

Signed...................................

Dated....................................

Annex 1G

Letter to client to explain home rights charge or restrictions

Dear [*name of client*]

I am writing to you further to our meeting as I have now obtained the necessary information from the Land Registry in respect of the property(ies) discussed in our last meeting.

It is clear to me now that [*name of spouse*] owns the family home at [*address of property*] in [his/her] sole name. As this property was [the family home/intended to be used as the family home] you are entitled to register your right to occupy the property. I can complete the form and send it to the Land Registry. When I do this the Land Registry will add a notice to the register. This means that for the duration of your marriage you are legally entitled to occupy the property. This right does not automatically give you any financial interest in the property, which could be established though the court proceedings.

Once the Decree Absolute/Final Order in the divorce/dissolution proceedings is pronounced you will lose your right to occupy the property. It is possible but rare for your right of occupation to be terminated by a court order.

I will complete the Land Registry form and lodge it with the Land Registry as soon as you authorise me to do so. You should be aware that [*name of spouse*] will be notified by the Land Registry that you have made this application. If you think that this is going to cause problems for you at home then we should discuss this matter before I send the form.

[*If the other party owns more than one property in their sole name, use this paragraph* – I have also obtained information that shows your spouse owns the following properties in [his/her] sole name:

1.
2.
3.

If possible we should register a restriction at the Land Registry against each of the above properties. This should ensure that if your spouse attempts to sell or charge these properties, any prospective buyer or lender is made aware that you have an interest in these properties. It doesn't necessarily prevent your spouse from selling the property, but you should be notified of any prospective sale and then we could make any necessary applications to the court to prevent a sale from completing.]

We can at the same time register a restriction against the family home so that your financial interest is protected as well as your right to occupy the property.

I look forward to hearing from you about this matter. If it is easier for you to do so please sign the bottom of this letter to indicate how you wish to proceed.

Yours sincerely

I [*name of client*] of [*address*] confirm that I have read your letter above and that I [would like/do not want] you to proceed to register a home rights notice against the property at [*address*].

[Additionally I would like you to register a restriction against the properties at:

1.
2.
3.   ]

I understand that [*name of spouse*] will receive notification from the Land Registry that I have made these applications.

....

Signed by [*name of client*]

[*date*]

2 Making a financial remedy application

2.1 Introduction

In this chapter we look at the essential matters that need to be considered when making an application to the court for financial remedies.

The precedent at **Annex 2A** gives a filled-in example of the standard financial remedy application that is used in all matrimonial and civil partnership breakdown cases. The precedent also provides a link to a blank version of the Form A; this is to ensure that the practitioner always has access to the most current version of the form. The form changes from time to time, but the information required remains essentially the same.

This form needs to be filed with the relevant issue fee or fee remission form at the Divorce Centre where the divorce petition was filed. The relevant court fee can be found using Form EX50 on HM Courts and Tribunals service website: **formfinder. hmctsformfinder.justice.gov.uk/ex50-eng.pdf**.

In the event that the divorce proceedings have been moved to a hearing centre for a costs hearing, then the Form A should be filed wherever the hearing was held.

Practitioners should note that the President of the Family Division stated in 2017 that he intended to separate the process of divorce and financial remedy. Although this had not been achieved at the time this toolkit went to print, a pilot project was underway at the Family Court in Southampton and the system was due to be taken nationwide in June 2017. The Form A will be issued at a separate court from the divorce which will remain at the Divorce Centre. Guidance will be issued by HM Courts & Tribunals Service (HMCTS) to assist practitioners.

The practitioner should note that either the petitioner or the respondent to the divorce is able to complete the form. This is possible as long as neither party has lost the right to make the financial remedy applications. Both parties retain the right to make financial remedy applications up until such time as they remarry. If the applications are not made before a party's remarriage then that party loses the right to make an application – this is known as the 'remarriage trap': Matrimonial Causes Act (MCA) 1973, s.28(3).

2.2 Completing Form A

The full names of both the applicant and respondent need to be completed on page 1.

2.2.1 Nature of application

Beneath the heading 'Nature of application' the applicant must tick one of the three available boxes. If the party applying has never previously made an application for financial remedy, for example in the divorce petition, the first box should be ticked – 'to apply to the court for'. This indicates that this is their application.

If the applicant previously indicated their intention to apply for financial remedy orders, either in the prayer of the petition or in a cross-petition or answer to the petition, then the second box should be ticked – 'to proceed with the application in the [application] [answer] for'. This indicates that they are proceeding with applications that were made in the petition, cross-petition or answer.

Note that the form uses the word 'application' rather than 'petition'.

There is a third box, which is used to apply to vary an existing financial remedy order under MCA 1973, s.31. These variation applications are limited to variations of periodical payment orders or lump sum orders payable in instalments only.

Once the applicant has ticked a box to indicate the nature of the application, the applicant must then indicate to the court which applications will be made. These fall into four broad categories:

1. Income orders.
2. Capital orders.
3. Property orders.
4. Pension orders.

There is only one application that can be made for an interim order, which is the first tick box, 'an order for maintenance pending suit/outcome of proceedings'. This box should only be ticked if the practitioner wishes to have an immediate hearing on the issue of interim maintenance. It is also sensible in that situation to highlight in the covering letter that a hearing is required, and an appropriate time estimate for that hearing should be indicated.

It is generally good practice to tick all the other boxes unless it is known in advance that there is no property against which a property adjustment order is being sought or pensions against which pension orders are being sought. If a property adjustment order is sought for one or more properties, the address of the property (or properties) should be set out where indicated.

It should also be noted that each party can make the same claims against the other. Although one party will be the first to issue, the other party should consider whether to make a cross-application for financial remedy. This might be necessary in order to proceed with their right to make financial remedy claims, or if they need to effect service on pension trustees or mortgage companies as an 'applicant'. A cross-application requires the respondent to complete the Form A with the fee and submit it to the court where the proceedings are timetabled. The court will seal the Form A but should not issue a second timetable for filing documents as the original timetable should be used.

2.2.2 Additional information

If this form is being completed to submit with a consent order, the relevant box at the end of page 1 should be ticked. The form should then be signed at page 10 and submitted to the court with a consent order and other supporting paperwork.

The rest of the form should only be completed if no consent order is being submitted and the application is being sent to court to commence the financial remedy process.

2.2.3 Financial applications for children

In certain limited situations, the court will have the power to make financial remedy orders in respect of children. If those circumstances exist, the relevant boxes should be ticked on page 2. Typically, the third box is ticked to indicate that there is no agreement between the parties, in which case the applicant needs to indicate how the court has jurisdiction to make an order. It should be easy to pick out from the list underneath tick box 3 which of the connections applies in each case. In high income cases it will be usual to make separate applications for child maintenance orders.

It should be noted that if the applicant is hoping to obtain maintenance in addition to child support as assessed by the Child Maintenance Service (CMS), then the CMS must have produced a maximum assessment calculation before making the application to the court. It is not enough for the parties to agree that the CMS will produce a maximum assessment calculation to confer jurisdiction for child maintenance on the court.

2.2.4 Applications relating to land

On page 2 the applicant is asked to indicate whether their application relates to land. This can be a property or a piece of land, either in England and Wales or overseas.

If the applicant indicates that their application does relate to land, details of any mortgagee should be entered in the indicated box.

2.2.5 Service details

On page 3 the applicant needs to indicate whether or not the applicant is represented by a solicitor in these proceedings. If the applicant is being represented on an unbundled retainer, box 2 should be ticked to indicate that the applicant is receiving advice but that their solicitor is not on record as acting for the applicant. If the solicitor is willing to go on record, the applicant should tick box 3 and complete the solicitor's details in the box immediately following.

A solicitor on the record receives all further correspondence from the court and is duty bound to deal with it, whereas a practitioner who is only advising does not.

2.2.6 Mediation information and assessment meeting

From page 4 onwards the information set out ensures that all applicants are aware of their obligation to attend a mediation information and assessment meeting (MIAM).

The applicant should complete section 2a, 2b or 2c to indicate whether an exemption from attendance is being claimed. There are two different types of exemption: the applicant may be exempt from attendance (2a) or the mediator may say that the applicant is exempt (2b). Finally, the applicant can indicate that the meeting has been attended (2c).

The MIAM should be held by a mediator who is authorised and trained to hold this meeting. The mediator will explain to the client the various non-court dispute resolution options available. The parties are not required to attend mediation but the applicant is required to attend a MIAM. The respondent will be invited to attend a MIAM by the mediator who conducts the applicant's MIAM. In rare cases a judge can order the respondent to attend a MIAM.

From page 5 onwards the applicant must indicate which of the relevant exemptions applies to their situation. Although the applicant is not required to submit any evidence of their purported exemption to the court, the applicant could be asked to produce evidence at the first hearing. In practice, this is rarely requested. The solicitor has regulatory obligations to the court and should not tick any boxes relating to any exemptions unless the solicitor has investigated the matter first and is satisfied that their client is indeed exempt.

On page 9, if box 2b was ticked on page 4, the mediator should indicate which of the mediation exemptions apply. The mediator can choose any option under 4a but should tick 4b if the applicant did attend the MIAM. It is very important that the mediator and no one else signs at the signature box on page 9 and that the mediator indicates their Family Mediation Council registration number.

Either the applicant or their solicitor (if on record as acting) should sign the signature box on page 10. A solicitor advising under an unbundled retainer should not sign this form as the applicant will be a litigant in person.

2.3 Service of the application on the respondent

Once the Form A has been sealed by the court it needs to be served on a number of people according to the Family Procedure Rules (FPR) 2010, SI 2010/2955.

According to FPR 2010, a copy of the sealed application should be sent to the respondent by a court officer within four days of the date on which the application was filed. In reality, it can take longer than four days for the court to issue the application and so the respondent may not receive their copy of the application as provided for in the rules.

Under FPR 2010, the applicant must also serve the respondent with a copy of the application and notice of the date of the first hearing. The rules state that the applicant must send a blank financial statement to the respondent and file a certificate of service at or before the first hearing. Typically, the court will serve the sealed Form A and blank financial statement on the respondent.

2.4 Third parties who can be served with a copy of the application

Other than the respondent, a limited number of people are entitled to receive a copy of the sealed application. FPR 2010, rule 9.13 states:

(1) Where an application for a financial remedy includes an application for an order for a variation of settlement, the applicant must serve copies of the application on –

(a) the trustees of the settlement;
(b) the settlor if living; and
(c) such other persons as the court directs.

(2) In the case of an application for an avoidance of disposition order, the applicant must serve copies of the application on the person in whose favour the disposition is alleged to have been made.
(3) Where an application for a financial remedy includes an application relating to land, the applicant must serve a copy of the application on any mortgagee of whom particulars are given in the application.

Where an application is made for pension sharing, FPR 2010, rule 9.31 states that a copy of the sealed application must be served on the person responsible for the pension arrangement (PRPA) concerned.

The requirements for service are slightly different where an application is made for a pension attachment order. FPR 2010, rule 9.33 states that a copy of the sealed application must be served on the PRPA concerned. However, the applicant is also required to send details of an address for service of notices on the applicant and an address to which payments to the applicant should be sent. In addition, if the applicant's bank details are given, sufficient information should be provided to ensure that the payment can be made into the applicant's account.

It should be noted that the PRPA has 21 days from the date of service to ask that the person with pension rights provide information disclosed in the financial statement in relation to those rights or benefits.

It should therefore be noted that no other persons can be served with a copy of the sealed application without specific permission being sought from the court.

Annex 2B is a standard letter to the mortgage company sending it a copy of the sealed Form A. Whilst there is no requirement for the mortgage company to confirm receipt of the letter, it is good practice to request this.

Annex 2C is a standard letter to the pension trustees sending them a copy of the sealed Form A. There is an additional paragraph that will need to be utilised in the event that an application for a pension attachment is made. This adheres to the requirements in FPR 2010. Practitioners should note that a standard letter needs to be sent in respect of each pension arrangement. It is good practice to obtain notification of receipt of the letter. Where the respondent makes a cross-application for financial remedy in order to make pension claims, the Form A should be served on the pension trustees in the usual way using this letter.

Practitioners should not forget to file a certificate of service with the court before the first appointment. There is a standard certificate of service form available on HMCTS website as Form FP6, see **formfinder.hmctsformfinder.justice.gov.uk/ fp6-eng.pdf**.

2.5 Notifying third parties about the application

Those third parties who cannot automatically be served with a copy of the sealed application may need to be notified about the existence of the application. The solicitor must be careful that no confidential information is accidentally revealed in the initial letter. **Annex 2D** is a letter to a third party informing them that financial proceedings have been issued by one of the parties to divorce proceedings, which can be adapted as appropriate.

A third party may be a joint owner of the property, may have an interest in the joint bank account or may allege that they have a beneficial interest in an asset owned by one of the parties to the divorce. The nature of a third party's interest should be specified in the precedent letter at para.2.

This letter should only be sent to a third party in the event that they purport to have a financial interest in assets that may be captured within the proceedings. An order from the court is required before the Form A can be served on the third party but advance notice by way of letter can be given. The third party may then take independent legal advice and decide that they want to be joined to the proceedings or that they want permission to intervene within the proceedings.

Annex 2A

Completed extract from Form A

Form A 'Notice of intention to proceed with an application for a financial order' can be viewed and downloaded at **formfinder.hmctsformfinder.justice.gov.uk/form-a-eng.pdf**.

The first four pages of Form A, completed as described in **Chapter 2**, are reproduced below.

Notice of [intention to proceed with] an application for a financial order

To be completed by the Applicant	
The Family Court sitting at	Case No.
	AB 1234567

Help with Fees – Ref no. (if applicable)

H W F – ☐☐☐ – ☐☐☐

Please note you must have previously filed a petition for a matrimonial or civil partnership order before completing this form. This form should only be completed if you are applying for one of the financial orders shown against the tick boxes below. If you are applying for a financial remedy other than a financial order in the Family Court please complete Form A1, unless you are applying for:

- financial relief after overseas divorce/dissolution etc under Part 3 of the Matrimonial and Family Proceedings Act 1984/Schedule 7 to the Civil Partnership Act 2004 (please complete D50F)
- financial provision under section 27 of the Matrimonial Causes Act 1973/Part 9 of Schedule 5 to the Civil Partnership Act 2004 (please complete D50C)
- alteration of a maintenance agreement under section 35 of the Matrimonial Causes Act 1973/paragraph 69 of Schedule 5 to the Civil Partnership Act 2004 (please complete D50H)

Full name of applicant

Subita Patel

Full name of respondent(s)

Suresh Patel

Nature of application

The Applicant intends:

- ☑ **to apply** to the Court for:
- ☐ **to proceed** with the application in the [application][answer] for:
- ☐ **to apply to vary**:

☐ an order for maintenance pending suit/ outcome of proceedings

☑ a secured provision order

☑ a lump sum order

☐ a property adjustment order
(please provide address, in the box below)

☑ a periodical payments order

☑ a pension sharing order

☑ a pension attachment order

☑ a pension compensation sharing order

☑ a pension compensation attachment order

Additional information required

Are you applying for an order by consent in terms of written agreement (a consent order)?   ☐ Yes   ☑ No   If Yes, **attach the draft order to this form**

Form A Notice of [intention to proceed with] an application for a financial order (06.16)   © Crown Copyright 2016

1. Further details of the financial application

Please tick the appropriate box below if an application is made for any periodical payments or secured periodical payments for children:

- ☐ and there is a written agreement made before 5 April 1993 about maintenance for the benefit of children
- ☐ and there is a written agreement made on or after 5 April 1993 about maintenance for the benefit of children
- ☑ but there is no agreement, tick any of the boxes below to show if you are applying for payment:

  - ☐ for a stepchild or stepchildren
  - ☐ in addition to child support maintenance already paid under a Child Support Agency assessment
  - ☑ to meet expenses arising from a child's disability
  - ☐ to meet expenses incurred by a child in being educated or training for work
  - ☐ when either the child **or** the person with care of the child **or** the absent parent of the child is not habitually resident in the United Kingdom
  - ☐ Other (please state)

Please tick the relevant box below to indicate whether this application for a financial order includes an application relating to land:

☐ Yes   ☑ No

If Yes, please provide details of any mortgagee(s) in the box below

2

Service details

☐   I am not represented by a solicitor in these proceedings

☑   I am not represented by a solicitor in these proceedings but am receiving advice from a solicitor

☐   I am represented by a solicitor in these proceedings, who has signed Section 5, and all documents
for my attention should be sent to my solicitor whose details are as follows:

Solicitor's details

Name of solicitor	
Name of firm	

Address to which all documents should be sent for service:	Telephone no.	
	Fax no.	
	DX no.	
	Your ref.	
Postcode ☐☐☐☐ ☐☐☐☐	Solicitor's fee account no.	

E-mail	

Respondent's address for service

Address (including postcode)
The Hill Walk
2 Hillside
Postcode A B 1 ☐ 2 3 K H

2. Requirement to attend a Mediation, Information and Assessment Meeting (MIAM)

Before making an application for a financial order you must first attend a Mediation, Information and Assessment Meeting (MIAM). At the MIAM an authorised family mediator will consider with you (and the other party if present) whether family mediation, or another form of non-court dispute resolution, would be a more appropriate alternative to court. The mediator will also be able to sign post you to other help and support services.

You **must** have attended a MIAM before making this application **unless** the requirement to attend a MIAM does not apply because the financial order you are applying for:

- is for a consent order; **or**
- you are exempt from the requirement to attend a MIAM. (Some exemptions you can claim for yourself, others must be certified by an authorised family mediator).

All applicants must complete sections 1 and 2 and complete and sign section 5 of this form. **In addition,** you must tick one of the boxes below and ensure that you, your legal adviser or a family mediator completes and signs the relevant section(s) of this form as shown.

2a. Are you claiming exemption from the requirement to attend a MIAM?	☐ Yes	☐ No	**If Yes, complete section 3.** **If No,** please **answer question 2b.**
2b. Has a family mediator informed you that a mediator's exemption applies, and you do not need to attend a MIAM?	☐ Yes	☐ No	**If Yes, you must ensure that the family mediator completes and signs section 4a.** **If No,** please **answer question 2c.**
2c. Have you attended a MIAM?	☑ Yes	☐ No	**If Yes,** you must ensure that the **family mediator completes and signs section 4b.** **If No,** you cannot make this application.

Annex 2B

Letter to mortgage company sending sealed Form A

Dear Sirs

Re: [*insert name and address of property or land charged*]

We represent [*name of client*] in [divorce] and matrimonial finance proceedings. Our client has made a financial application against the [property/land] detailed above.

We are required to notify you of our client's application as you have secured a mortgage against this [property/land]. We enclose a copy of our client's sealed application for your attention.

We should be grateful if you would acknowledge that you have received this letter so that we may confirm to the Court that we have complied with our obligation to notify you.

Yours faithfully

Annex 2C
Letter to pension trustees sending sealed Form A

Dear Sirs

Re: [*insert name of pension member, National Insurance number, date of birth and pension plan number*]

We represent [*name of client*] in [divorce and] matrimonial finance proceedings. Our client has issued a financial application against the person with the pension detailed above. The financial applications made include those for a pension sharing order, a pension attachment order and compensation orders if these are applicable to this pension scheme.

We are required to notify you of our client's application, and as such we enclose a copy of our client's sealed application for your attention.

[*Additional paragraph to be included where an application has been made for a pension attachment order:* The address where notices should be sent to the applicant is [*address*] and any payments ordered by the Court should be sent to the applicant at [*insert payment details*].]

We should be grateful if you would acknowledge that you have received this letter so that we may confirm to the Court that we have complied with our obligation to notify you.

Yours faithfully

Annex 2D

Letter to a third party advising them about financial remedy proceedings

Dear Sirs

Re: [*insert names of the parties to a divorce*]

We represent [*name of client*] in [divorce and] matrimonial finance proceedings. Our client has issued a financial application against [*name of spouse*].

We understand that you have an interest in the parties' financial affairs as [*explain in detail the third party's potential interest*]. Our client therefore puts you on notice that [he/she] has made a financial application in the Family Court at [*insert name of court*]. The proceedings have been issued under case reference [*insert case number*].

Should you wish to assert your right over [*insert details of potential third party rights that may be affected by a financial remedy order*] you should take immediate independent legal advice. You should let your legal adviser know that the [first/next] hearing in this matter is the [first appointment/financial dispute resolution hearing/directions appointment] and you may wish to put forward your case about [*insert details of potential third party rights*] before that hearing takes place.

We are not able to give you any advice in respect of this matter, but would suggest that you see a specialist family law solicitor. If you do not have a family law solicitor, you can find one by using the Law Society 'find a solicitor' function at **www.lawsociety.org.uk**.

Yours faithfully

3 Disclosure

3.1 Introduction

This chapter deals with the thorny issue of disclosure. This takes up a great deal of a practitioner's time in one way or another. The exchange of financial information will hopefully lead to the parties being able to negotiate a settlement. If the parties are unable to negotiate terms of settlement, the court should have sufficient information and documentation available to impose a financial division between the parties. The parties are usually able to reach a settlement at or after the financial dispute resolution (FDR) hearing.

3.2 Voluntary disclosure

Most solicitors will, at one time or another, agree to proceed with the process of 'voluntary disclosure'. This term is often used by solicitors without much precision and this can lead to confusion and ultimately additional expense for the client.

In the Law Society's *Family Law Protocol* it is correctly noted that the pre-application protocol is annexed to FPR Practice Direction 9A, where it has been since April 2011. The protocol indicates that solicitors should bear in mind the advantage of having a court timetable and a court-managed process. The process of voluntarily exchanging financial information is not automatically the best process to use in every case.

If it appears that there are any issues that may need outside determination, by either a judge or an arbitrator, then the practitioner needs to consider the risk of duplicated effort in conducting disclosure both outside and within the procedures.

The protocol also states that solicitors 'should bear in mind the objective of controlling costs and in particular the costs of discovery'. Sometimes practitioners suggest the voluntary exchange process without properly assessing the benefits of doing so and whether the costs will be proportionate.

The protocol goes on to state that 'the option of pre-application disclosure and negotiation has risks of excessive and uncontrolled expenditure and delay. This option should only be encouraged where both parties agree to follow this route and disclosure is not likely to be an issue or has been adequately dealt with in mediation or otherwise.' The precedent letters provide for a very tightly controlled timetable which can be altered according to the parties' circumstances. It is important that all parties adhere to the agreed timetable to ensure that there is no unnecessary delay.

This option is not dealt with in **Chapter 1** of this toolkit as it seems to fit better as a pre-litigation consideration. It is similarly dealt with in this way in the Family Law Protocol. Too many practitioners fail to consider non-court dispute resolution processes because they believe that the process of voluntary disclosure works in all cases. The practitioner should carefully consider the benefits of each process for each client.

Paragraphs 7 and 12 of the pre-action protocol deal with the issue of disclosure. There is an obligation on both parties to make full and frank disclosure of all material facts, documents and other information. The practical method of disclosure is not prescribed, although many practitioners believe that both parties must complete the Form E and exchange it together with all mandatory filing documentation. Paragraph 12 states that 'if parties carry out voluntary disclosure before the issue of proceedings the parties should exchange schedules of assets, income, liabilities and other material facts, using the financial statement as a guide to the format of the disclosure. Documents should only be disclosed to the extent that they are required by the financial statement. Excessive or disproportionate costs should not be incurred.'

In **Annex 3A** we have provided for two possible alternatives in respect of disclosure. In the first instance, we have asked the client to complete financial disclosure by way of the Form E. Although this can be time-consuming and may be costly for the client if assistance is needed to complete the form, if voluntary disclosure does not result in a settlement the Form E can be updated for the court process.

In the alternative provision, the precedent asks the client to provide the solicitor with the documentation required to produce schedules, rather than to complete the Form E. In cases where there is little money and the cost of full disclosure by the Form E would be seen to be excessive, it may be more sensible for the parties to exchange schedules of assets, liabilities, income and outgoings with select and relevant documents.

It is very important that practitioners are clear with each other from the outset what the format of disclosure will be and the documents they will be attaching to their schedules.

Annex 3B sets out the mandatory filing documents that a client is required to attach to the Form E; however, in reality the practitioner should try to tailor the requirements by deleting any documents that are not relevant.

3.3 Documents needed for Form E

Annex 3B sets out all of those documents that the client must produce when completing the Form E. As these documents must be filed when completing the form for litigation purposes, none of the items should be deleted, unless they have no direct application to the client. For example, if the client is not a business owner then box 2.11 can be deleted. The documents to be returned to the practitioner should be marked on the attached table and the client has space to make comments next to each box. If the client is waiting for a cash equivalent (CE) value of a pension, a note of the date when the request was sent to the pension trustee can be given at section 2.13. It can be quite difficult to control documents if they are sent to the practitioner in disorganised or piecemeal fashion, and so encouraging the client to send the paperwork in one batch is quite important.

Occasionally, the practitioner will be aware of other documents that are important in a particular case. For example, if there are two properties, one of which will be set out at section 2.2, there may be a deed of declaration of trust that must be provided. The practitioner should adapt the table to ensure that additional documents are requested in respect of each section if they are aware that such documents exist.

3.4 Self-help

It is very important that clients are told at an early stage of litigation that they should not 'help themselves' to their ex-spouse's documents. Even in cases where the parties have been fairly easy-going during the marriage about accessing documents, the client needs to be warned that this should stop when divorce proceedings are started.

The leading case in this area is the Court of Appeal decision in *Tchenguiz* v. *Imerman*; *Imerman* v. *Imerman* [2010] EWCA Civ 908. The Law Society's *Family Law Protocol* indicates at para.10.7.2 that it is a breach of confidence for one spouse to examine, copy, retain or use a confidential document.

The Court of Appeal described confidential documents as 'communications which are concerned with an individual's private life, including his personal finances, personal business dealings, and (possibly) his other business dealings are the stuff of personal confidentiality'.

A document will be confidential if one spouse knows that the other would not want them to look at the document or have a copy of it. Simply put, one spouse should not look at documents belonging to the other unless they have been given permission to do so, for example, if the parties have exchanged documents at mediation or during the collaborative law process. The fact that the parties had previously given each other permission to look at documents cannot be relied upon if their relationship has broken down and it should be clear that such permission is withdrawn.

It is, therefore, sensible to write to the other side to withdraw such permissions given by your client. If one spouse gave the other permission to access their online banking, email accounts or other online documents then permission should specifically be withdrawn to avoid any suggestion that permission to access those documents remains post-divorce. The letter at **Annex 3C** explains to clients that they should not give the practitioner any documents belonging to their spouse and explains the reasons why. A number of statutes prevent one party accessing the other's documents, for example, the Data Protection Act 1998, the Computer Misuse Act 1990 and the Postal Services Act 2000.

Where the client is concerned that their spouse will destroy documents before producing the Form E, the letter invites the client to discuss matters with the solicitor. There is a possibility that an application can be made to prevent the destruction of documents.

The best course of action is to prompt the client to change their online passwords and to ensure that they sever any iCloud or similar links with their ex-spouse's mobile devices. Although the spouse should not be looking at those documents, it is better to ensure that there is no access to them in the first place.

If the client gives the solicitor documents that do not belong to the client, the solicitor should immediately return the documents to their owner. The solicitor should not examine the documents or take a copy of them. Full disclosure of those documents should then be requested in the proper way during the proceedings.

3.5 Form E

The financial statement sets out the disclosure that the client is required to provide to the court. At the time of writing, changes to the Form E are anticipated as a result of the final report produced by the Financial Remedies Working Group (FRWG). It is proposed that the Form E in its current format be combined with the Form E1 and the Form E2 to create a combined document. Although a draft combined form was produced with the interim report of the FRWG, no final version has been introduced. Form E is available online at **formfinder.hmctsformfinder.justice.gov. uk/form-e-eng.pdf**.

3.5.1 Page one

The first page of the financial statement requires the important factual information such as the names of the parties, their role within the proceedings and the date of the form.

The warning notices on the first page are very important and the client's attention should be drawn to these notices when sending the form to the client to complete. Of particular relevance is the fact that any person found to have been deliberately untruthful may have criminal proceedings brought against them under the Fraud Act 2006. The warnings also outline that proceedings for contempt of court may be brought against a person who causes to a false statement to be made in a document verified by a statement of truth. In reality, it is extremely rare for criminal proceedings or contempt proceedings to be brought against a person who has deliberately lied on this financial statement.

In view of that warning, some clients will expect the court to act on inaccuracies or falsehoods or for there to be a sanction but the practitioner, knowing this to be unlikely, should manage that expectation.

There is a list of mandatory documents that should be filed outlined in **Annex 3B**. It is important to note that the client may attach other documents to the Form E where it is necessary to explain or clarify any information within the form. It is also good practice to include documents where these would aid understanding and clarify the content of the form and the overall financial picture of the client.

3.5.2 General information

The general information required on page 2 is fairly straightforward and these sections should not be left blank. Under MCA 1973, s.25(2)(d) the court is required to take into account the age of the parties and the length of the marriage. The practitioner should note that any period of cohabitation that has moved seamlessly to marriage will count towards the overall length of the marriage. Page 2 does not require any information to be inserted about the length of cohabitation, and this information should be inserted at section 4.5.

Clients sometimes express concerns about sections 1.8 and 1.9 regarding new partners or possible cohabitation in the next six months. Naturally, clients should be encouraged to be as honest as possible about their plans for the future. There is no definition of cohabitation in the Family Court, and practitioners should take careful instructions about their client's living arrangements. If the client suddenly commences cohabitation very soon after a financial settlement, the other party may make an application to set aside the order if that party believes there has not been full and frank financial disclosure of pertinent facts.

Details of any children of the family are usually limited at section 1.10 to minor children who were children of the family, i.e. lived together with the parties of the marriage. It is, however, possible to include details of adult children, particularly where they continue to reside with one of the parties and are being supported by them.

When giving details of the state of health of the client or the children, consideration should be given to any documents that could be attached in order to clarify any health conditions. It is good practice to give detailed information about any medication that is being taken to manage the health condition and whether any tests or diagnosis are imminent. This will minimise the enquiries raised at the questionnaire stage.

If expert medical evidence is needed this will be directed by the court.

MCA 1973, s.25(2)(e) requires the court to take into account any mental or physical disability of either party. It is therefore important that sufficient information is given to the court to enable this exercise to take place.

The court needs to understand the educational arrangements for the children, and this can include tertiary education for soon-to-be adult children. Although the court does not need to prioritise the welfare needs of adult children, their needs will not be wholly discounted. If the schools are fee-paying then it is worth mentioning that fact here.

If you are completing the form for the spouse who is to pay child maintenance, it is prudent to undertake a CMS calculation using the relevant website: **www.gov.uk/ calculate-your-child-maintenance**.

If you are acting for the person receiving child maintenance, the sum actually being paid should be inserted or if the parties are living together an indication of the sums or specific bills being paid by the paying party should be given. It can be unhelpful if section 1.13 is left blank or if the receiving party indicates that they are not receiving maintenance if, for example, their bills are being paid instead of a formal payment of child maintenance.

Where the application before the court is to vary a previous order, section 1.14 requires the previous order to be attached together with clarification of the parts that require variation. It should be noted that MCA 1973, s.31 deals with the variation of financial remedy orders; these are restricted to periodical payments orders or lump sum orders payable in instalments.

In section 1.15, insert details of any other court cases in England and Wales or abroad involving the parties. Any criminal proceedings should be detailed here.

In section 1.16, the present residence of the client is required together with details of the occupation of that property; for example, is the client a joint owner of the property, living with parents, or living in the property under a licence or a tenancy agreement? If there is a tenancy agreement, it may be prudent to attach a copy of that agreement to the financial statement.

3.5.3 Financial details

Part 1 Real property (land and buildings) and personal assets

Section 2.1: the client should complete any information about the family home. If the property has been sold and the proceeds of sale are being held in an account, this information should be inserted elsewhere.

Although it is not mandatory to file the office copy entries from the Land Registry, it is good practice to do so. Section 2.1 requires details of the Land Registry title number and details of the mortgage company, both of which can be obtained from the Land Registry.

Details of who owns the property will be recorded on the Land Registry title but it may be that the client advises you that the beneficial interests are different. For example, the parties may have entered into a deed of declaration of trust and the client believes it reflects the beneficial interests rather than the legal title. In this case, the client's instructions should be carefully recorded and the deed should be attached to the Form E.

It is possible that the client will reveal a potential third party interest at this stage and, if so, this should be drawn to the attention of the court in the statement of issues. The court might join a third party to the proceedings if it is relevant to do so.

It is not uncommon for the client to hold the property with their spouse as joint tenants but to give instructions that the beneficial interests are held unequally. The practitioner should tread carefully in these cases, as it is not usual to set those arguments out on this page. The client may wish to detail any contributions to the property purchase at section 4.3 rather than set out different beneficial interests at section 2.1.

The client should obtain an up-to-date mortgage redemption statement so that the correct figures can be inserted on this page together with any penalties that would fall due for an early redemption. It is possible that early advice from an independent financial adviser or a mortgage broker would be helpful at this stage, if there is a hope that the mortgage will be transferred to the client. Mortgage lending criteria have changed drastically in the last five years and it is important to know whether the client can afford to take over the mortgage debt. It is possible that the client will not be permitted to take over the mortgage at all and, if so, this information needs to be found out sooner rather than later.

Property valuation

The valuation of the family home can be a thorny issue. If both parties live in the property they should both be able to obtain independent estate agents' valuations. If one party is excluded from the property either voluntarily or by order of the court, it may be difficult to obtain an accurate valuation. Caution should be exercised when using online valuation tools as they are not particularly accurate. It may be possible to ask an estate agent to conduct a 'drive-by' valuation which is probably more accurate than an online tool. There is always a difference between a marketing price and the realistic sale price of a property and the client should be told this to manage their expectations.

Neither party should go to the expense of paying for a valuation at this stage as the costs are unlikely to be recoverable; a sole party expert is not likely to be used in these proceedings. It is important that both parties have an approximate idea of the value of the property as, other than their pension, this is likely to be the most valuable asset that they own.

The estimate of the costs of sale is usually a fixed percentage of the current market value of the property. Depending on the geographical location and preference of the local court, this figure can be anywhere between 2% and 3%. The total equity in the property is calculated by deducting the costs of sale and the balance outstanding on any mortgage together with penalties. The equity should be divided equally between the parties in the event that they are joint owners with no other declaration of trust.

If there is a deed of declaration of trust than it is perfectly acceptable to divide the equity between the parties in accordance with that document. Practitioners should note that it is unlikely that the court will ring-fence and exclude any assets according to a deed of declaration of trust as MCA 1973, s.25 requires the court to balance all resources available to each party.

Section 2.2 is similar to section 2.1 but this pertains to other property, land or buildings either in England and Wales or abroad. This is where the details of, for example, a holiday home rental property can be input using the same guidelines as above. If Capital Gains Tax (CGT) is payable on the sale or transfer of a second property, this information should be input at section 2.10.

Section 2.3 requires clients to complete information about all bank and building society accounts that they have in their sole name, in joint names with another person or that they have held in the last 12 months but have recently closed. This also includes an account that they have a beneficial interest in. For example, if a client regularly places money in another person's account but considers the money to be theirs, the client should declare the beneficial interest.

Often parents have bank accounts on behalf of their children but the accounts are actually held in the parents' names. These accounts should be disclosed in section 2.3 but in 'the total current value of your interest' section the answer will be nil if the beneficial interest of the proceeds of the account belongs to the child and not the parent. An example is shown in Table 3.1.

Table 3.1 Example of completed section 2.3

Name of bank or building society, including branch name	Type of account (e.g. current)	Account number	Name of other account holder (if applicable)	Balance at the date of this statement	Total current value of your interest
Santander – Wimbledon branch	Savings account for Maria Jones	1234567	N/A	£34,500	Nil
Santander – Wimbledon branch	Current account	9876543	N/A	£1,278	£1,278
Santander – Wimbledon branch	Savings account	6758493	Stefan Jones	£2,000	£1,000

In the case of each account careful consideration should be given to the final column, 'the total current value of your interest'. It may be that in the case of joint accounts, one party has not had access to the account for some time and therefore the balance of the account belongs to the other party. Full instructions should be taken on this point.

Section 2.4 can be quite complicated depending on the type of investments the client discloses. The paperwork associated with this section is limited to the latest statement or dividend counterfoil in respect of each investment. If the client has an investment manager, they may be able to supply a letter that outlines the investments and any particular risk/liquidity issues in connection with them. Not all investments are liquid and this will not be immediately apparent from the information required to be input at section 2.4, or even the documentation attached to that section.

Clients usually have straightforward investments, such as listed shares or ISAs and these can be easily bought and sold subject to market variations.

Section 2.5: the client should provide all information in respect of any life insurance or endowment policy held. It may be that the practitioner needs to cross-check the information given by the client against the direct debits from their bank account to ensure that all policies have been disclosed. It is good practice to obtain a letter from the insurance company to confirm that a policy has no surrender value to ensure that clear disclosure is given.

It is sensible to get an experienced independent financial adviser involved in financial planning at an early stage, particularly where there are life policies that may be kept or surrendered. Practitioners cannot give financial advice and so before any settlement is proposed the client will need to understand the financial consequences from a person who is authorised to give advice.

Section 2.6: if clients are owed any money this should be detailed here, and it is a good idea to cross-check their bank statements to ensure that they have not 'loaned' any friends or family large sums of money that do not appear in this section. If there is a loan agreement, this should be attached to the financial statement; however, it is more likely that any loans are soft debts and this should be made clear.

Section 2.7: it is not unusual for some people to hold large sums of cash and this must be disclosed.

Section 2.8 can be a little tricky if the client has personal possessions that are very valuable. At this stage, the client is only required to identify those possessions and to give an estimate of the value. Any individual items that are worth less than £500 on resale should be excluded. Valuations are required for the sale of the item second hand, not when bought as new.

If an individual item forms part of a collection that is worth more than £500, then the collection should be valued and included. Ordinarily, items of furniture and house contents are not individually worth more than £500, and it is not cost proportionate to obtain valuations for house clearance at this stage.

The client should not go to the expense of paying for an expert valuation as this is something that may need to be addressed at the first appointment and a single joint expert (SJE) instructed. It is unusual to be involved in cases that require an expert opinion in relation to section 2.8.

The client should provide values only for their chattels and not for their spouse's. There will be an opportunity to challenge their spouse's chattels valuations later in the proceedings, although it is rarely cost proportionate to do so.

Part 2 Capital: Liabilities and Capital Gains Tax

Section 2.9: the client is required to set out all debts owed, excluding the mortgage and overdrawn bank and building society accounts which are included elsewhere in the form.

The client should set out the nature of the liability, details of the other account holder if applicable and the total liability owed. In the final column 'total current value of your interest in the liability' there are a number of different responses that can be given.

When parties enter into a credit agreement they are each responsible for the whole debt. They may attribute the liability in shares between themselves but this does not bind the lender. This means that in respect of a joint liability the strict position is that each party is responsible for the whole debt. Often, the client does not wish to appear to take on responsibility for the whole debt in the financial statement. It may be that a note needs to be made in this section to set out the client's position, which is that the parties had always paid the liability in specified shares and that the client believes that the client should only be held responsible for a share of the debt.

In the alternative, the client could complete the final column 'total current value of your interest in the liability' to reflect the sum that the client believes is their responsibility and which reflects the agreement between the spouses. An example is shown in Table 3.2.

Table 3.2 Examples of completed section 2.9

Liability	Name of other account holder (if applicable)	Total liability	Total current value of your interest in the liability
DFS sofa loan	My spouse	£5,000	£2,500
DFS sofa loan	My spouse	£5,000	£5,000[*]
DFS sofa loan	My spouse	£5,000	£1,000

[*] Although I am liable for this debt, the sofa is in my ex-spouse's home. I have no access to the sofa and I don't think I should be held responsible to repay this debt. The monthly repayments are currently being paid from the joint account.

In the first entry in Table 3.2 the client has given instructions that the client should only be responsible for half of the total liability because they believe this is fair.

In the second entry the client accepts the legal position, which is that the client is responsible for the whole debt. However there is a note that gives reasons why they do not believe they should be responsible for the debt.

In the third entry the client has given instructions that the client is only responsible for £1,000 of the debt as this is what had been verbally agreed with the spouse when the sofa was purchased.

Any of these is potentially acceptable as long as there is an explanation at section 2.9, otherwise there are likely to be questions raised by the other party about the distribution of this joint liability.

Capital Gains Tax payable needs to be identified at section 2.10. It is sensible to list those assets that would incur a CGT liability if sold or transferred. In the case of real property, it may be a good idea to obtain a CGT calculation from an accountant.

If there is a complex portfolio of investments, the investment manager will usually be able to calculate CGT due if the portfolio is sold or transferred.

If there is a dispute about the CGT liability it is possible that an SJE will be needed to advise on CGT; thus it is initially sensible to get a calculation carried out.

Part 3 Capital: Business assets and directorships

Section 2.11 requires the client to complete details of any business interests: this relates to sole traders, partnerships and limited company interests. In each case it is mandatory to attach business accounts for the last two financial years, to the extent that they exist. As sole traders do not need to file accounts it may be that their paperwork is limited to their income tax returns, with no formal accounts.

A business valuation will be needed; however, in many income-producing businesses there is no inherent value to the business itself. Clients should provide any information they can. If they have an accountant, a letter from that accountant should suffice to support any valuation. It is not necessary to spend any money obtaining a formal valuation at this stage, because if there is any dispute as to the value of the business a single joint expert will be appointed.

If there is any CGT to pay, the accountant should estimate the amount and the information should be inserted in this section. If the client does not have sufficient information to complete this section, the client should contact an accountant. It is not the solicitor's job to decipher the client's business dealings.

If the company is a limited company, quite a lot of information is available for free via the Companies House website, at **www.gov.uk/government/organisations/companies-house**. It is a good idea to check this website for information about your clients' companies or those of their spouses.

Section 2.12 is easily completed by the practitioner, who can access the Companies House website and undertake a director's search without charge.

Part 4 Capital: Pensions and Pension Protection Fund (PPF) compensation

The issue of pensions can be a daunting one for practitioners, but the information required in the Form E is fairly straightforward. Section 2.13 should be completed for each pension that the client has, and this should be totalled to a final composite figure.

Since the introduction of the single-tier pension, it is sensible to obtain a valuation for this using Form BR19 (**www.gov.uk/government/publications/application-for-a-state-pension-statement**). Technically, this is an application for a state pension statement which is not mandatory and does not need to be included as a section

2.13 page. However, this is very useful information for the practitioner and the statement should be attached to the Form E.

Under the new state pension regime, the Additional State Pension (SERPS) and the State Second Pension no longer exist. It is still possible to get a valuation for divorce purposes – see **www.gov.uk/government/uploads/system/uploads/attachment_ data/file/526327/br20.pdf**. This information will not necessarily assist the pension expert, even though the Form E requires the client to obtain the information.

When completing the valuation requests in respect of state pension schemes, it is important to note whether the petition was filed before 6 April 2016 or after that date. The client should be specifically advised to put the date of the petition in the form, otherwise the Department for Work and Pensions will assume that the petition was issued after 6 April 2016 when the new scheme came into effect.

All other pensions should be included and any pension that is being administered by the Pension Protection Fund (or is in the PPF assessment period); the client should be aware if their pension has been taken on by the PPF. The PPF keeps a full list of pensions have been transferred to it – see **www.pensionprotectionfund.org. uk/Pages/homepage.aspx**.

The client should contact the pension trustees or the board of the PPF as soon as possible so that there is enough time to obtain the CE value. Many schemes can take three months to produce a CE valuation and so it is imperative that early enquiries are made.

When the information is returned by the pension trustees for the PPF, it should be possible to complete section 2.13 with full information. The information provided for divorce purposes will indicate whether the occupational pension is paying reduced CEs. This is also true of underfunded schemes, where the trustees must offer shadow membership as an implementation option.

The pension valuations should always be dated within the last 12 months; if not, a further valuation should be requested. Most pension schemes will provide one CE without cost every 12 months. If the member is drawing the pension, or is within 12 months of doing so, the administrators may charge for providing the CE.

There is sometimes a misconception that a pension in payment cannot have a valuation, but this is not the case. Often, it will cost the member to obtain a CE for a pension in payment. These costs can be quite high, particularly for government pension schemes.

If the pension valuation is not available when the Form E is completed, the information should be obtained as soon as possible and filed with the court and the other side when it is received. FPR 2010, rule 9.14 states that if a party is unavoidably prevented from sending a document required by the financial statement, i.e. the pension valuation, that party must send a copy of the document to the other party and the court as soon as possible. When the document is sent to the court, the party must provide a written explanation of the failure to send that document with the financial statement. This is an important provision which is often overlooked by practitioners.

Part 5 Capital: Other assets

Section 2.14 is an all-encompassing section, covering any other investments or assets that have not yet been disclosed. The list at the beginning of the section is not exhaustive and clients should be reminded that any asset, interest in a trust or anything of value in England and Wales or abroad should be included. It may be that the client is the beneficiary of a discretionary trust and that this information will need to be input. Once again, if there is an investment manager who is able to assist in the preparation of the Form E, then the manager's advice should be sought at an early stage.

Sometimes clients will want to know whether they need to include an inheritance that they may come into in the future. Generally speaking, if testators are still alive then there is no guarantee that their wills will remain the same until death. There is also no guarantee that there will be any money in the estate at the point of death. However, if somebody is the ultimate beneficiary of a will trust then this is something that should be disclosed.

Part 6 Income: Earned income from employment

The information in section 2.15 can be completed using the P60 and the last three payslips, which must be filed with the Form E in any event. If the client works shift patterns, the most recent payslips will assist in calculating an average monthly sum that the client is paid. This will help to ascertain the future net income in the next 12 months and whether there is any surplus income at the end of the month after the payment of outgoings.

Using the client's payslips, an explanation should be provided as to any additional deductions, for example for travel expenses or pension contributions. If the payslips are not an accurate reflection of the normal income then a full explanation should be given. If there are any bonuses or other occasional payments these should also be indicated as an accurate picture of the client's income is needed. It is most important in this part of the form to provide an accurate estimate of the net income in this employment for in this next 12 months. If the figure is significantly different from the net income figure for the last 12 months, whether higher or lower, full explanation needs to be given in box 4.1.2, but this is sometimes forgotten by practitioners. For example, if the client has recently started, or is about to start, a new job, this may be an explanation for a change in estimated net income.

If the client has disclosed a business interest in a limited company, the client will often be receiving a small income which represents their director's remuneration. The majority of their income from that company will be received by way of dividend payments on their shares.

Part 7 Income: Income from self-employment or partnership

Even if clients have already disclosed a business interest, they will still need to complete section 2.16 of the Form E to disclose their income from that business.

Once again, this section can probably be completed by their accountant. A copy of the last tax assessment will be needed to ascertain the client's tax liability.

Ordinarily, the last tax return rather than the tax assessment is attached. Often, if only the tax assessment is attached, the other side will ask for a copy of the last tax return to ensure that all income has been declared. It is important to estimate the net annual income for the next 12 months as accurately as possible. If the figure is different from the previous year's net income, an explanation should be given on page 15 where requested.

Part 8 Income: Income from investments

In section 2.17 the practitioner must cross-reference the earlier sections of the Form E which may have referred to income-producing investments (sections 2.2, 2.4 and 2.14). Clients often forget to disclose the income from these investments and this can lead to further questions being raised in the questionnaire. Although no further evidence needs to be provided to support the additional income, there is likely to be evidence of deposits into the disclosed bank statements. It is important to provide an accurate estimate of income for the next 12 months. If there is an investment manager dealing with a portfolio of investments, the manager may be able to give an estimate of investment income.

Clients should not forget to disclose any income from a second property, or even from renting a room in their property.

Part 9 Income: Income from state benefits

When completing section 2.18 it is important to note that tax credits are not classified as state benefits, as they are paid by HMRC not the benefits agency. If the client is entitled to child benefit, disability living allowance or state pension payments these should be included together with any other benefits.

Part 10 Income: Any other income

Income from a private pension or compensation received from the PPF should be included in section 2.19. Often there is documentary evidence to support these payments and although it is not mandatory to file that information, it is good practice to do so.

All tax credits can be inserted into this section.

If the client is receiving child maintenance, this should be included here. It may have been mentioned in section 1.13 but the income sections calculate the complete net income figure and the information in earlier sections is therefore not included.

If the client is receiving housekeeping money from an adult child, this should be included here. Any other income, royalties for example, not previously disclosed should be disclosed in this section and an estimated net income figure for the next 12 months should be provided.

Although the form suggests that figures can be given gross or net, it is much more helpful for net figures to be used throughout.

Summaries

If the practitioner is using good Form E software, the summaries page will self-calculate. If the practitioner is using the Form E provided at **formfinder.hmcts formfinder.justice.gov.uk/form-e-eng.pdf** then sections 2.20 and 2.21 should be carefully added up to ensure that the calculations are correct. The summary pages are not particularly useful in practice, but do need to be correct. There is a precedent schedule of assets at **Annex 3J** that can be used for hearings and for the purpose of settlement negotiations rather than relying on the summary pages.

3.5.4 Financial requirements

Part 1 Income needs

Section 3.1 requires the client to indicate whether income needs are being set out as weekly, monthly or annual figures. It does not matter which the client uses but the periods should be consistent. Most practitioners set out monthly figures rather than weekly or annual figures.

In the section starting, 'I anticipate my income needs are going to change because' the client should insert an explanation as to how their current costs and estimated future costs are likely to differ. For example, the client may currently be in rented accommodation and hope to be able to purchase a house after the financial remedy proceedings have concluded.

It may be that the client is housed in a property that is too big for their current needs and so the client is likely to sell the property and purchase a smaller property which should be cheaper to maintain. A realistic approach needs to be taken in this section and when setting out the estimate of income needs at section 3.1.1.

If the client does not wish to move from the current home, current and estimated future costs will not vary greatly. It may be that some items of expenditure will change due to natural price increases, such as the cost of petrol, electricity and gas. The client may, for example, be on a fixed-rate mortgage deal which is due to come to an end in the next 6 to 12 months and a new estimate may be provided for mortgage payments thereafter. The client must be able to justify any difference between the two columns at section 3.1.1.

The Excel spreadsheet at **Annex 3D** sets out an easy-to-follow format for the client to complete. This is presented as a spreadsheet rather than a Word document as this will be much easier for the practitioner to amend/update as the case goes on.

Annex 3D is divided into five sections:

A   Housing expenses.
B   Other home expenses (these are maintenance expenses rather than the mandatory provision of utilities, etc.).
C   Vehicle expenses (these are limited to the expenses associated with owning a vehicle).
D   Personal expenses (these include all personal items including entertainment and work expenses if there are any).
E   Expenses for children (these represent the information required in section 3.1.2).

Each subsection is totalled in respect of both current and estimated future costs. There is also a total for the client's expenses and a grand total to include all income needs. The grand total figure is the sum that should be inserted on page 20 of the Form E.

Any additional items can be added to the schedule to ensure that it is appropriate for the client and the children. The schedule will be the basis for any maintenance claim, or if completed by the paying party will inform the court whether there is any surplus income once their outgoings have been paid.

Practitioners should be aware of the impact of this exercise and use their experience to discourage the use of unrealistic figures – either too high or too modest. The budget is intended to inform the court and so needs to be as accurate as possible.

Part 2 Capital needs

Section 3.2 requires the client to complete information about capital needs for themselves and for their children (if any). Capital needs are primarily centred on housing and any improvement to housing that is needed. Therefore the main item in section 3.2.1 will be a property to live in. It is a good idea to indicate the size of property being sought and the geographical location in which that property is required. Often the client would like to remain living in the property that was the family home; if so, this is usually input together with a value of the family home.

In the event that a different property will be required for housing, the additional costs of purchase and stamp duty and moving will need to be included. If the new property needs renovating, furnishing and carpeting, these costs should be included.

Occasionally there are other capital needs, for example, cost of a car or other equipment that is necessary for the client.

Capital needs for children are limited; however, school fees might be paid from capital and therefore included at section 3.2.2 rather than at 3.1.2. Sometimes children have capital needs for sports equipment or equipment to support a disability. If there is a need or desire for one parent to assist an adult child to pay university tuition fees this should be included here.

3.5.5 Other information

General

The information in section 4 should be completed very carefully as this is the information that the court will use to assess the merits of the claim. Naturally, as the litigation progresses, information can be expanded upon if directions are given to allow the filing of statements or the additional filing of evidence. However, practitioners should use these sections to ensure that all of the information that they hope to rely on is included from the outset. This means that detailed instructions need to be taken about all of the matters included.

Many of the items covered in this section correlate to MCA 1973, s.25; therefore, it is imperative that the information is as full as possible.

Section 4.1.1 asks the client to detail any significant changes in assets or income in the last 12 months. If capital has been utilised for legitimate reasons, for example the payment of legal costs, then it is fully transparent to include those capital payments in this section. If income has increased or decreased in the last 12 months, this is the place to include that information and provide any evidence if it assists.

Likewise, any anticipated changes in assets or income in the next 12 months should be detailed at section 4.1.2. Thus, for example, if the client is likely to drawdown a pension lump sum then this must be highlighted so that appropriate safeguards can be put in place, if necessary, to prevent a disposition of this money. If there is likely to be a significant change in income in the next 12 months, this may have been noted at section 2.15 and a full explanation can be given here.

Standard of living

Section 4.2 reflects MCA 1973, s.25(2)(c). This requires the court to take into account the standard of living enjoyed by the family before the breakdown of the marriage. Whether your client is a high net worth individual or someone with average assets and income, this section must be completed. The following phrases are often seen in this section:

> 'The parties lived a fair standard of living, they both worked during their marriage and claimed child benefit and tax credits. They were able to enjoy a caravan holiday every year and have not been abroad since before the children were born.'

Or perhaps if the parties enjoyed a better standard of living this may be typical:

> 'The parties enjoyed a very good standard of living as the wife has a very well paid job. Husband has not needed to work and has stayed at home with the children of the family. The parties enjoy three foreign holidays a year, a skiing holiday in the winter, a beach holiday in the summer and at least one city break during the year. The children both attend private fee-paying schools. The parties have a cleaner and gardener and enjoy the use of a part-time cook during the week.'

Contributions

Section 4.3 deals with any particular contributions that one party has made to the family property and assets or outgoings or to family life or to the welfare of the family. This section reflects MCA 1973, s.25(2)(f), which states that the court must have regard to 'the contributions which each of the parties has made or is likely in the foreseeable future to make to the welfare of the family, including any contribution by looking after the home or caring for the family'.

It may be that one party wishes to emphasise financial contributions made to the purchase of the family home. The asset is disclosed at section 2.1 but if it is owned in joint tenancy, the equity will be divided equally at total A. The client may wish to persuade the court that the equity should not be distributed in accordance with legal ownership, so this section needs to be completed in full. If the client has any evidence to support this position, this evidence should be attached to the Form E otherwise further questions will be raised in the questionnaire about the financial contributions.

This section should be completed in light of the House of Lords judgment in the case of *White* v. *White* [2000] UKHL 54. This case indicates that although the parties to the marriage may have different roles – often one is the wage earner and the other is the homemaker – their contributions will be treated as equal even though these contributions are of a different nature.

The court will look at one party's contributions and may distribute the assets to take those contributions into account.

Conduct

Section 4.4 should only be completed by the client in rare circumstances. This section mirrors MCA 1973, s.25(2)(g), which says that the court must have regard to 'the conduct of each of the parties, if that conduct is such that it would in the opinion of the court be inequitable to disregard it'.

The leading case on conduct is *Miller* v. *Miller; McFarlane* v. *McFarlane* [2006] UKHL 24. This identifies that the conduct argument should be used in only the most exceptional cases. In those cases the conduct will be 'obvious and gross'.

Mere domestic violence will not meet the criteria for conduct even if such violence is sufficient to prove unreasonable behaviour in a petition for divorce. Financial misconduct may be sufficient to meet the criteria in this section.

If this section is completed frivolously then it can lead to accusations that the maker of the statement has embarked on a course of litigation conduct. District judges do not take kindly to these sections being completed when they should not. Clients should be made aware of the serious consequences of completing this section improperly.

Any other circumstances

Section 4.5 allows the client to include any other circumstances that have not yet been mentioned that may significantly affect the extent of financial provision. This reflects the provision at MCA 1973, s.25(1): the court shall have regard to all of the circumstances of the case.

There is a list of matters that may be applicable and anything that the client has not yet covered can be input here. We mentioned above that any significant period of premarital cohabitation should be mentioned here.

Section 4.6 specifically asks for information about the client's new relationship, if any, and asks for information about the new partner's income, assets and liabilities. It is helpful for the client to provide this information, as failure to do so can heighten distrust between the parties, which will impact negatively on the possibility of settling matters.

3.5.6 Order sought

It may be too soon to be able to complete this section but the practitioner should attempt to present a transparent position for the client.

If the client hopes to remain in the family home, this should be stated in section 5.1(a) so that proper directions can be given to investigate the possibility of releasing the other party from any mortgage covenants. It should be made clear if a sale of the family home is sought.

The practitioner should know whether continuing spousal maintenance is sought (section 5.1(b)), even if it is too soon to know if there is sufficient income to meet this need.

If there has been no pre-litigation disclosure, the client might not have sufficient information regarding their spouse's pension situation when answering section 5.1(c). Therefore the answer to this section might be a little more vague.

Section 5.2 relates to applications for a variation of an ante-nuptial or post-nuptial settlement and, if such a variation is sought, the settlement needs to be identified.

If there is an application for an avoidance of disposition order, section 5.3 needs to be completed to identify the property to which the disposition relates. In such cases the party to whom the disposition was made must be served with a copy of the application and they can request a copy of the financial statement within 14 days of service (FPR 2010, rule 9.13(4)).

3.5.7 Statement of truth

Although the statement of truth can be signed by the solicitor, it is preferable if it is signed by the client. FPR 2010, Part 17 and Practice Direction 17A deal with the practice rules regarding statements of truth.

Paragraph 3.8 of Practice Direction 17A states that where a legal representative signs the statement of truth, this signature will be taken by the court as the legal representative's statement that the legal representative has authority to sign the statement of truth. The practitioner should be careful to obtain authority before signing the Form E.

It is also an indication that the practitioner explained to the client that in signing the statement of truth, the client was confirming that it was the client's belief that the facts in the document were true.

The practitioner will also be taken to have explained the possible consequences if it subsequently appears that the client did not have an honest belief in the truth of those facts.

3.5.8 Schedule of documents to accompany the Form E

These documents are the mandatory filing documents that the client is required to submit. It is good practice to complete this page to indicate which documents are attached.

However, in addition to completing this section it is good practice to produce an index page appended to the front of the documents. This sets out the documents attached, the sections that the documents relate to and the date(s) of the documents.

This practice accords with the provisions of FPR 2010, Practice Direction 22A, para.11.3: 'Where an exhibit contains more than one document, a front page should be attached setting out a list of the documents contained in the exhibit. The list should contain the dates of the documents.'

Annex 3B includes a template for the list of documents that should accompany the Form E.

3.6 Schedule of outgoings

It is important for every practitioner to have access to a good schedule of outgoings to give the client as a precedent. Therefore **Annex 3D** is an Excel spreadsheet for the client to complete or for the solicitor to complete with the client. Many schedule of outgoings documents are created as Word documents, which may be easier for the client to complete than an Excel spreadsheet. However, using a spreadsheet will make it easier to update the information if the client's situation changes.

Annex 3E simply provides a letter enclosing the Form E to be sent to the court; this can also be adapted to send to the other side. It should be noted that if any mandatory filing documents cannot be sent with the Form E, it is good practice to mention this when sending the form.

3.7 After the exchange of Form E

The letter at **Annex 3F** sets out those matters that should be explained to clients when sending them their spouse's Form E. Obviously, there is a limited time within which to prepare the following documents:

1. Request for further information and documentation, otherwise known as 'the questionnaire'.
2. Statement of issues.
3. Chronology.
4. Form G (this indicates whether the parties are in a position to use the first directions appointment as a financial dispute resolution hearing).

Generally, the solicitor can start to draft the documents without any input from the client; however, the client's input will be needed before the documentation can be exchanged with the other side.

3.8 Statement of issues

Annex 3G provides an example of a statement of issues. There is no specified format, and each judge in each court will have a different preference. It seems sensible to set out any issues between the parties with reference to the sections of Form E so that there is a certain logic to the document.

The court will be interested in any relevant disputed issues between the parties. This will inform the judge what directions will need to be dealt with at the hearing.

3.9 Questionnaire

FPR 2010, rule 9.14(5) states that a questionnaire must be prepared, setting out by reference to the statement of issues any further information and documents requested from the other side. Generally speaking, only one document is prepared, which is referred to as 'the questionnaire'. This incorporates a request for information from the other side by way of a narrative response, and documentation that the other side is required to produce.

The practitioner should be very careful when drafting the questionnaire to ensure that it is very clear whether information or documents, or both, is required.

Occasionally no questions need to be raised and if this is the case the parties are probably ready to use the first appointment as a dispute resolution hearing.

Cross-examination questions should not be asked in the questionnaire. The purpose of this document is to complete or clarify disclosure.

Any directions sought or valuations needed should be mentioned in the statement of issues and not raised as questions in the questionnaire.

It is important that the statement of issues lays the groundwork for the questions that are raised in the questionnaire. For example, **Annex 3G** indicates that the other party has raised issues about the child of the family's medical conditions. The client does not agree that these medical conditions exist. In **Annex 3H** questions are raised about the health of the child of the family. These are requests for both narrative information and documentation.

Sometimes issues are raised in the statement of issues but there are no corresponding questions. For example, **Annex 3G** indicates that the other party would like the child of the family to continue at the fee-paying school currently attended. The client states that this may not be affordable in the future. Clearly this is a matter for the court to decide on, and there are no relevant questions that will assist the court at this stage.

The practitioner should be very careful to ensure that the questions are relevant and to reference the statement of issues.

3.10 Chronology

The chronology needs to be filed with the statement of issues and questionnaire. A precedent is shown at **Annex 3I**, so it can be seen that this is drafted in a neutral style. Practitioners sometimes insert contentious matters which are not necessary.

Essentially, the court needs to have an overview of the important dates in the parties' relationship. Any contentious matters can be raised in a position statement filed before the hearing.

3.11 Schedule of assets

Annex 3J provides a schedule of assets in an Excel format for the practitioner to use throughout the proceedings. The earliest point at which it can be prepared is once the Form E documents have been exchanged. This is an extremely effective way of keeping an overview of the assets in the case. It can be submitted to the court at each hearing and utilised when sending offers to settle. An up-to-date schedule ensures that all the assets are accounted for and properly dealt with in the financial settlement.

The schedule is different from the summaries page of the Form E as the pensions valuations are not added to the investments and real property sections. Pensions should be treated as illiquid assets and presented in an asset schedule in a separate section. Although pensions can sometimes be viewed as liquid assets, it is good practice to treat them separately.

The precedent has a summary section:

1. total property;
2. total investments;
3. total personal possessions;

4. items 1 to 3 above are added together to give a total for liquid assets;
5. total pensions, both in payment and those not in payment;
6. total debts;
7. net assets are calculated as item 4 minus item 6 (pensions are not included in this calculation).

Net income figures are collated for both husband and wife so that their income positions are clear and comparable.

3.12 Conclusion

This chapter covers a lot of ground regarding disclosure obligations before the first hearing when disclosure is the main focus of preparation. The duty of full and frank disclosure to the court is ongoing and this should be kept in mind by the practitioner and client.

Annex 3A

Letter explaining information required for voluntary disclosure

Dear [*name of client*]

Voluntary disclosure

As you know we have agreed with [*name of spouse*]'s solicitor that we are going to proceed with 'voluntary disclosure'. Disclosure is the process whereby each party collects their financial information for the purpose of swapping that information with the other party. We have agreed to do this and then try to negotiate a settlement. If this process works there will be no need to start court proceedings. We will, however, need to send a draft consent order to the court for the judge to approve the terms of settlement. The judge has the power to accept or reject a settlement. If the settlement is fair to both parties, the judge will accept it and make an order.

One of the potential pitfalls of proceeding with voluntary disclosure is that the parties sometimes take a very long time to prepare the financial information needed. Obviously, the longer you take to give me your financial information, the longer it will be before negotiations can start.

Timetable

In order to proceed with voluntary disclosure it is important that you understand that although there is no specific timetable to adhere to, it is important that we try to exchange financial information as quickly as possible.

If we were to proceed with litigation, we would have 8 to 12 weeks to complete the financial disclosure form, known as the 'Form E'. In this case, I think that it is sensible to try to exchange financial information with [*name of spouse or solicitor*] within an [8] week period. In my experience, if we take a long time preparing the financial information, any drive to move negotiations on may be lost.

A: Form E disclosure

In this case we have agreed to exchange financial information by using the Form E as a guide. I have therefore enclosed a blank copy of the Form E for your attention. You should complete each section of the Form E and return the form to me together with the evidence you are required to attach to each section. Some sections will not be relevant and so you can ignore them.

If you have any questions or queries about the form please do not hesitate to contact me for further guidance.

[If the practitioner has agreed to exchange financial information by way of schedules with supporting documents, it is sensible to send the following to the client.]

B: *Disclosure by schedules*

Please would you obtain the following information for voluntary disclosure by way of schedules.

(a) I need to have detailed information about your income from all sources, including dividend payments, rental income, PAYE income, tax credits, benefits, pensions and all other income sources. Additionally, I need to have your last P60 and evidence of your income as disclosed.

(b) I need information regarding all of your bank accounts, whether they are held in your sole name or jointly with another person. I need to have 12 months' bank statements for each account.

(c) I need information regarding all of your savings and investments if they are held outside bank accounts, together with evidence of those investments and any income derived from them.

(d) I need the address of each property that you own in your name either solely or with another person. I also need to know the value of such property and details of any mortgage or charge secured against property with the current statement showing the total amount to repay that debt. If you own any property or land overseas, you should include that property in your disclosure.

(e) I need to know details of any partnership or limited company that you have an interest in together with a value of that business interest. If you have a business accountant he/she may be able to assist you in obtaining a valuation. I will also need to have the last two years' accounts for each business that you have an interest in.

(f) If you have any debts, you should provide me with a list of those debts and any documentary evidence to show the outstanding sum owing. Debts could include money owing to a bank or building society, money owed on HP agreement or money owed to credit or store cards. I would recommend that you provide me with at least (3)/(6) months' statements for each debt.

(g) I need you to complete the attached schedule of outgoings document, as this will help me to understand how much money you need on a monthly basis. We can discuss the content of this document after you have prepared it to ensure that the information that you have given is accurate.

(h) If there is any other information relating to your financial or personal circumstances, you should let me have this information as soon as possible. For example, if you are living with someone, then I need to know this, and I will need information on their financial position to disclose to the other side. In addition, if you are about to receive an inheritance, that is relevant and I need to have detailed information regarding this.

(i) If you have an interest in a pension, you will need to obtain a cash equivalent valuation (CEv) for the pension. The pension trustees who administer your pension will be able to provide you with a CEv. Please note that it can sometimes take six weeks or more to obtain the CEv and so you should contact your pension trustees as soon as possible.

Pension valuations

Usually there is no charge for obtaining the CEv as the trustees are obliged to provide you with one valuation per year without charge. Sometimes, if you are approaching retirement age they will charge for the provision of this information. If there is a charge, you must pay it to obtain the information as no settlement is likely to take place without this information.

If you are already receiving an income from your pension, I still need to have the CEv but you will definitely be charged by the pension trustees for this information. It is important that you obtain the information as there is not likely to be a settlement of these matters until we have the valuation information.

Once you are able to give me all this information, I will prepare the [Form E] [schedules] needed to send to the other side. When I obtain their financial information I will send this to you. I would like to arrange for us to have a meeting where we can discuss if there is any more information needed or whether we can proceed to negotiate with the information we have.

If you have any questions or queries please not hesitate to contact me.

Yours sincerely

Annex 3B

Letter explaining to the client the documents required for Form E

Dear [*name of client*]

As you are aware, you are required to complete the financial Form E and file it with the court by [*date*]. You already have a blank Form E which you are starting to complete. To help you to remember to send the relevant documentation I have prepared an easy-to-complete table which is attached. Please fill this out to indicate which documents you have sent me, whether you have applied for the document from a third party or whether you have no documents for that section.

I would much prefer it if you send me all of the paperwork at the same time. This is to ensure that I can use my time efficiently to go through the Form E and all supporting documents. It can increase your costs if you send me paperwork in a piecemeal fashion as it means that I will need to look at the paperwork on multiple occasions, for which you will be charged. I would like you to send me the Form E and documents by [*date*] so that we can finalise it before the filing date.

If you have any questions, please contact me to discuss these.

Yours sincerely

Form E section	Document required	Sent	Notes
2.1	Please provide me with a copy of any valuation you have for this property.	Yes/no	
	Mortgage redemption figure for each mortgage secured against this property.	Yes/no	
2.2	Please provide me with a copy of any valuation you have for this property.	Yes/no	
	Mortgage redemption figure for each mortgage secured against this property.	Yes/no	
2.3	Please provide 12 months' statements for each bank account you have set out in this section.	Yes/no	
2.4	For all savings and investments, please provide the most recent dividend document or the most recent statement.	Yes/no	
2.5	If you have any life insurance or endowment policies, I will need to see the paperwork in respect of each policy. If the policy has a value, you should provide me with a document showing the current value for that policy.	Yes/no	

Form E section	Document required	Sent	Notes
2.11	Please provide your last two years' business accounts and any document that supports the valuation you give for the business. A letter from your accountant should be sufficient. There is no need to go to the expense of obtaining a formal valuation.	Yes/no	
2.13	I need to know the cash equivalent value for each pension in your name. You can obtain this valuation from the pension trustees who administer your pension fund.	Yes/no	
	Please make the request for a valuation as quickly as possible as this can sometimes take several weeks or months to obtain.	Date requested from trustees:	
	Please note that it is a good idea to obtain a state pension valuation by completing Form BR19.	Yes/no	
	You may also have additional rights under the previous state pension and so you should complete Form BR20 to find out what the valuation of this is.	Yes/no	
2.15	Please provide your last P60.	Yes/no	
	Please provide your last three payslips.	Yes/no	
	Please provide your last P11D if you have one.	Yes/no/not applicable	
2.16	I need to have your last tax assessment. If you do not have this, a letter from your accountant confirming your tax liability will be sufficient.	Yes/no	
	If your net income from the last financial year and your estimated net income for the next 12 months are different, I need to have a copy of management accounts for the period since your last account.	Yes/no/not applicable	
3.1	Please complete the attached schedule of outgoings for you [and the child(ren)]	Yes/no	

Annex 3C

Letter to client explaining disclosure requirements, self-help and online protection

Dear [*name of client*]

As you are aware, it is important that both you and [*name of spouse*] provide full frank and clear financial information about your individual and joint circumstances. This obligation is often referred to as 'disclosure'. You need to provide ongoing information about your personal and financial circumstances as these will have an impact on any settlement prospects and court proceedings.

The duty to provide disclosure is owed to your spouse but principally to the court. If you are not sure whether to tell me about a change in your circumstances then you should err on the side of safety and let me know.

Failure to give full disclosure

If you do not give me information which is later found out, it is possible that any order made will be set aside. This means that you may need to go through the financial disclosure process again and a different order could be made. This can lead to a duplication in legal costs and costs orders could be made against you. It is also possible that you will lose credibility if it is discovered that you have failed to give full and frank disclosure.

Accessing your spouse's documents

There is often a concern that your spouse will not be as open and honest as you will be in these proceedings. This concern might possibly tempt you to help yourself to [*name of spouse*]'s documents. The courts are very strict about accessing documents that do not belong to you. **Please do not access or give me any documents that belong to [*name of spouse*]**. If you access and give me [*name of spouse*]'s documents when you should not have done, I may not be able to represent you any further in these proceedings and the court might impose strict penalties on you for doing so.

If [*name of spouse*] has shared financial information and documentation with you in the past and you still have access to that information now, you may be able to obtain copies of the documents and share them with me. However, if you know that [*name of spouse*] would not want you to have those documents, you should not give me copies of them.

You should not access any of [*name of spouse*]'s personal communications at all. For example, this would include personal letters or emails from friends or family members.

Online protection

I am aware that couples often share passwords and documents electronically with each other. I would recommend that you change all of your passwords immediately.

I would also recommend that you sever any iCloud accounts or cloud-based software if it is connected to any devices held by your spouse. It is sometimes easy to forget that any documents you save on your laptop might be uploading to your spouse's mobile devices. I would therefore recommend that you carry out a thorough check of your online activity to ensure that your spouse has no access.

Likewise, you should not access [*name of spouse*]'s documents or online activity that you may legitimately have had access to in the past. This means that even if they forget to change their passwords or accidently leave you with access to their documents, you should not access them. You should be aware that, if you were to illegally access [*name of spouse*]'s documents on their computer, criminal sanctions could be imposed upon you.

If you think that [*name of spouse*] will destroy documents as a result of these proceedings we could apply to the court to stop [him/her] from doing so. Please discuss this issue with me if you think that important documents are going to be destroyed and I can advise you further.

If you have information belonging to [*name of spouse*] that you think is important, please speak to me about this first **without** sending me the documents.

Yours faithfully

Annex 3D
Schedule of expenditure of applicant/respondent

Item	Current (£)	Future (£)
A Housing		
Mortgage/rent		
Council tax		
Buildings insurance		
Contents insurance		
Gas		
Electricity		
Oil		
Water		
Home telephone		
Mobile telephone		
Broadband		
Home TV package		
Netflix		
TV licence		
Replacement furniture		
Replacement white goods		
Total A:		
B Other home expenses		
Boiler cover		
Cleaner		
Gardener		
Window cleaner		
Food shopping		
Total B:		
C Vehicle expenses		
Car loan/lease/HP costs		
Car tax		
Car insurance		

Item	Current (£)	Future (£)
Petrol		
Maintenance service and MOT costs		
AA/RAC		
Depreciation		
Total C:		
D *Personal expenses*		
Clothes		
Dry cleaning		
Shoes		
Accessories		
Hairdressing		
Beautician		
Cosmetics		
Optician		
Dentist		
Medical insurance		
Dental insurance		
Entertainment (meals out/ theatre/cinema/etc.)		
Books/music		
Gym		
Holidays		
Christmas expenses		
Birthday expenses		
Pension contributions		
Life insurance		
Endowment policy		
Savings		
Work lunches		
Train travel		
Parking costs		
Amazon Prime, etc.		

Item	Current (£)	Future (£)
Total D:		
E Expenses for children		
School fees		
Childcare costs		
Clothes		
Shoes		
Hairdressing		
School uniform		
Sports kit		
School trips		
Tuition fees		
Magazines		
Health insurance		
Club memberships		
Entertainment		
Pocket money		
Holiday		
Total E:		
Total for self (A–D):		
GRAND TOTAL (A–E):		

Annex 3E

Letter enclosing Form E to the other side and the court

Dear Sirs

RE: [*names of parties and case reference number*]

We enclose the Form E on behalf of the [applicant/respondent] in this matter. We confirm that we have filed a copy of the Form E with the [Court/other side].

The [applicant/respondent] has been unavoidably prevented from attaching to the form the following document[s].

1.
2.
3.

These will be sent to the [applicant/respondent/court] as soon as they are available.

Yours faithfully

Annex 3F

Letter enclosing other party's Form E and next steps

Dear [*name of client*]

I am pleased to confirm that I have received [*name of spouse*]'s financial statement. I enclose a copy of it for your attention.

You might find it daunting to look through the statement and the documents attached but I would ask that you read everything carefully. I will be going through the financial statement myself so that we can prepare documents to file with the Court before the hearing on [*date*].

The Court will allow us to ask questions about [*name of spouse*]'s financial disclosure before the hearing. We are permitted to ask [him/her]:

1. To clarify any matters in the statement.
2. To identify any unusual transactions in their bank or credit statements.
3. To ask about assets that we think might be missing.

I would therefore like you to look through the financial statement and documents to identify any of the following:

(a) Unusual bank transactions. These might be payments to someone you don't recognise, recurring direct debit payments, credits from sources you don't recognise or transfers to accounts you don't recognise.
(b) Assets that you think are missing from the disclosure. This may be a personal possession such as a car or jewellery, or it might be an investment that used to exist but that doesn't appear in the financial statement.
(c) Anything in the statement that you think is untrue or incorrect.
(d) Anything in the financial statement or supporting documents that you would like more information about.

Questionnaire

I will then prepare a document called a request for further information and documentation, also known as 'the questionnaire'. I will send you this document in a draft format so that you can see which documents we are asking [*name of spouse*] to produce and the questions we are asking [him/her] to answer.

The Judge at the first appointment will decide whether we are allowed to receive the information we want from [*name of spouse*].

We are not likely to get another opportunity to ask [*name of spouse*] questions until the final hearing and so we should make sure we ask all the relevant questions now.

Statement of issues

I also need to prepare a document called the statement of issues. This document sets out the areas of dis/agreement between you. This helps the Judge at the first appointment to decide which questions should be answered to help the process along.

Once I have drafted the statement of issues I will send it to you for your final approval.

Chronology

I am obliged to prepare a document called the chronology. This is simply a list of important dates and events. It gives the Judge an overview of your relationship with [*name of spouse*].

I will send you a draft of this document for your final approval.

First appointment

As you know we need to attend the first appointment on [*date of hearing*]. I will write to you before the hearing to let you know what to expect. For the time being, we are preparing the paperwork to submit on [*date*].

Please contact me to give me your views on [*name of spouse*]'s disclosure so that I can start to draft the above paperwork.

Yours sincerely

Annex 3G

Statement of issues

IN THE FAMILY COURT AT [*location*]

CASE No:

IN THE MATTER OF THE MATRIMONIAL CAUSES ACT 1973

BETWEEN:

[Name of applicant] **Applicant**

– and –

[Name of respondent] **Respondent**

[Applicant/Respondent] Statement of Issues

1.11 Health

The applicant/respondent has indicated that the child of the family has medical conditions. The applicant/respondent does not agree.

1.12 Educational arrangements

The applicant/respondent has indicated that the child of the family will continue to attend the same private fee-paying school. The applicant/respondent does not believe that this will be affordable in the future.

2.1 Family home

The applicant/respondent has provided a valuation for the family home which is unsupported by evidence. The applicant/respondent does not accept that the valuation given is accurate.

Dated: ....

[*Name of solicitors*]

[*Address of solicitors*]

Annex 3H

Request for further information and documents – 'the questionnaire'

IN THE FAMILY COURT AT [*location*]

CASE No:

IN THE MATTER OF THE MATRIMONIAL CAUSES ACT 1973

BETWEEN:

[Name of applicant]   **Applicant**

– and –

[Name of respondent]   **Respondent**

[Applicant/Respondent] Request for further information and documents/ questionnaire

1.11   Health
1. The [applicant/respondent] is asked to produce evidence that the child of the family suffers from the medical conditions listed.
2. [He/she] should also provide a narrative explanation of when these conditions were first diagnosed.

2.1
3. Can the applicant/respondent produce a signed copy of the deed of declaration of trust referred to in this section?

Dated: ....

[*Name of solicitors*]

[*Address of solicitors*]

Annex 31

Chronology

IN THE FAMILY COURT AT [*location*]

CASE No:

IN THE MATTER OF THE MATRIMONIAL CAUSES ACT 1973
BETWEEN:

[Name of applicant] **Applicant**

– and –

[Name of respondent] **Respondent**

[Applicant/Respondent] Chronology

Date	Event
dd.mm.yyyy	Husband born (current age: [*age*])
	Wife born (current age: [*age*])
	Parties meet
	Parties commence cohabitation
	Parties' son [*name*] born (current age: [*age*])
	Date of marriage (X year relationship)
	Parties' daughter [*name*] born (current age: [*age*])
	Date of separation
	Date of petition
	Decree Nisi
	Husband/wife applies for financial remedies
	Husband/wife cross-applies for financial remedies
	Sealed Form A served on mortgagee and pension trustees
	Husband/Wife Form E signed
	Husband/Wife Form E signed
	Husband/Wife Statement of issues, questionnaire, chronology
	First appointment

Dated: ....

[*Name of solicitors*]

[*Address of solicitors*]

Annex 3J

Schedule of assets

[Insert name of parties]

[Insert date of hearing]

		Joint (£)	Husband (£)	Wife (£)
PROPERTY				
Family home *[Address]*	Value			
	Mortgage			
	Penalty charges			
	Costs of sale 2.5%			
	Net equity			
2nd property *[Address]*	Value			
	Mortgage			
	Penalty charges			
	Costs of sale 2.5%			
	Net equity			
Total net equity:				
INVESTMENTS				
Husband's	Bank account			
	Bank account			
	Bank account			
	ISA			
	ISA			
	Shares			
	Portfolio of investments			

		Joint (£)	Husband (£)	Wife (£)
Wife's	Bank account			
	Bank account			
	Bank account			
	ISA			
	ISA			
	Bonds			
	Unit trust			
Total savings:				
PERSONAL ITEMS				
Husband's	Car			
	Watch collection			
Wife's	Car			
	Diamond ring			
Total personal items:				
PENSIONS				
Husband's	Pension 1 (*CE dated*)			
	Pension 2 (*CE dated*)			
	Pension 3 (*CE dated*)			
Wife's	Pension 1 (*CE dated*)			
	Pension 2 (*CE dated*)			
Total pensions:				
DEBTS				
Husband's	Credit card			
	Car loan			
	Legal fees outstanding			
	Legal fees loan			
Wife's	Store card			
	Money owed to father			
	Litigation loan			

		Joint (£)	Husband (£)	Wife (£)
Total debts:				
SUMMARIES				
Total property				
Total investments				
Total personal possessions				
Total:				
Total pensions				
Total debts				
Net assets (excluding pension):				
INCOME				
Husband's	PAYE			
	Dividends			
	Rental income			
Wife's	PAYE			
	CMS			
	Tax credits			
	Child benefit			
Net income (PCM/PA):				

4 First directions appointment

4.1 Introduction

The precedents in this chapter are designed to deal with all matters up to and including the first directions appointment (FDA, or first appointment). The FDA is usually the point in time when the court will appoint experts if a proper application has been made in accordance with FPR 2010, Part 25.

Once the Form E, questionnaires, statement of issues and chronologies have been exchanged and filed with the court, the practitioner should ensure that the client is aware of the next steps.

4.2 Choice of advocate

Prior to the first directions appointment, clients should be able to choose the person they would like to represent them at the hearing. It may be that the practitioner does not undertake advocacy but there is another person within the firm who is able to take this on, rather than engaging counsel. **Annex 4A** offers the practitioner a number of choices:

1. the practitioner undertakes the advocacy themselves at their usual hourly rate;
2. another person within the firm undertakes advocacy at their usual hourly rate;
3. a barrister is instructed to deal with the case on a fixed fee;
4. additionally, it is possible that a junior from the firm may be sent to the hearing to assist the barrister and their costs also charged to the client.

The practitioner should ensure that advocacy fees are paid in advance, particularly where a barrister is instructed. It is ordinary practice for family barristers to charge a 'deemed fee' for abortive preparation work and for possibly turning away other work due to the scheduled hearing. This means that if the case settles before the hearing or is taken out of the list by the court the barrister will be able to charge all or part of their fee. Counsel's clerk will usually inform the practitioner of any deemed fee arrangements when counsel is booked; however, it is good practice to check the deemed fee dates and diarise them.

It is also worth explaining to the client who will be responsible for preparing bundles, particularly if the applicant is a litigant in person and responsibility falls upon the respondent. FPR 2010, Practice Direction 27A sets out the rules for bundle preparation.

If the other party is a litigant in person, the client should be told that the client may not have a legal representative at the hearing. Instead, clients may ask for a friend to accompany them to the hearing. Usually no formal applications are made before the hearing but such a request will often be made at the hearing. The Law Society's practice note on dealing with litigants in person contains invaluable information for practitioners.

4.3 Form H Estimate of costs (financial remedy)

Form H Estimate of costs (financial remedy) is available online at **formfinder. hmctsformfinder.justice.gov.uk/form-h-eng.pdf**. It is very straightforward and needs to be filed by each party at the first appointment (FPR 2010, rule 9.27). It is interesting to note that there is no specific requirement that each party must exchange their costs estimate with the other party, only that they produce the costs estimate at the hearing. Although it is commonplace for parties to exchange estimates of costs with each other when filing questionnaires and statements of issues, there is no procedure rule that requires this to take place.

The first page of the estimate of costs takes into account the items on page 2. Section A deals with those costs incurred in financial remedy proceedings prior to the issue of Form A. This generally means the practitioner's costs of advising during any non-court dispute resolution processes. Any previous solicitor's costs should be included at boxes 1 and 3, the current solicitor's costs should be included at boxes 2 and 4, and counsel's fees at box 5.

If the client is paying privately the second column marked 'indemnity rate' should be completed; clients in receipt of legal aid should complete column one.

Part 2 is only required in respect of private client costs incurred by a legally aided client.

Section B requires the practitioner to detail those costs incurred after the issue of Form A. As above, the costs and disbursements incurred by a previous solicitor should be separated from those incurred by the current solicitor. The solicitor should ensure that these costs include representation to the date of the first appointment.

A good case management system will allow the practitioner to easily complete this form and calculate the sum that has been paid towards the outstanding costs. This figure must be inserted on page 1.

4.4 Statement of costs (summary assessment)

FPR 2010, Practice Direction 28A states at para.4.5 that if a party seeks a costs order against another party, this should be made plain in open correspondence or in skeleton arguments before the date of the hearing. Where a summary assessment of costs is appropriate the parties should file a statement of costs using Form N260.

Form N260 is available online at **formfinder.hmctsformfinder.justice.gov.uk/n260-eng.pdf**. This form must be completed and served on the other side no less than 24 hours before the date of the hearing. The form must be signed by a partner at the firm of solicitors, or a director of an LLP.

On the first page details of the practitioner should be inserted. These should include their level of qualification/training and their associated grade derived from that. The box at the end of page 3 sets out the various grades and levels of qualification.

The form should be completed to indicate the attendances on the client, experts, counsel, court and any other party. An estimate of the time spent attending the hearing should be inserted if a representative from the firm is attending; otherwise, counsel's fees can be inserted at page 4.

Any other expenses such as the initial court fee and any disbursements incurred at the Land Registry or elsewhere should be inserted under the heading 'other expenses'. The correct rate of VAT should be applied and a grand total of all costs should appear on page 4. The grand total should not exceed the maximum sum of costs chargeable to the client: this is known as the indemnity principle.

4.5 Post-hearing action

As soon as the practitioner receives a copy of the sealed order from the court, this should be sent to the client. In practice, the advocate would be responsible for preparing the order and the client may have taken the order away with them at the end of the hearing. It may be, therefore, that the practitioner is writing to the client to explain an order which the client already possesses.

It is of course important to take clients through the order to ensure that they understand what they need to do and when they need to supply the practitioner with any information or documentation.

The letter at **Annex 4B** assumes that the questionnaire was amended by the judge and that the client has the amended questionnaire. The answers to the questionnaire need to be signed by the client with a statement of truth. This is often overlooked by practitioners: FPR 2010, Practice Direction 9A, para.5.2.

This precedent assumes that the parties are given the opportunity to agree the valuation of the family home and in default will choose a valuation expert, who will be an estate agent or a RICS surveyor. It is usually incumbent upon the practitioner to choose the valuer and it is therefore useful to have details of a number of good local valuers to hand. Valuers whose estimates have proven inaccurate in past cases or who have earned a reputation such that the local judges habitually disregard them should be avoided.

Likewise if a pension expert is to be instructed, it is useful to have details of a number of suitably qualified actuaries or financial planners available. Resolution has a very good accreditation scheme for IFAs and many of these could be used to prepare a pension report.

4.6 Instructing an expert

Annexes 4C, 4D, 4E and **4F** all relate to the instruction of an expert. The letters have common themes: it is useful to inform the expert whether there are court proceedings ongoing and, if so, which court, or whether their expertise is required to assist in non-court dispute resolution processes. If the parties agree to instruct an expert on a joint basis, this is perfectly acceptable in the absence of a court order. The expert should be instructed to prepare a report which would comply with evidential rules and be acceptable to a court even if no financial remedy proceedings have been commenced.

Each of the letters has a central box for contact details. This is to ensure that the expert can easily contact the parties' solicitors when needed.

The background information in each letter gives a little more detail about any order of the court which should be enclosed with the letter of instruction. FPR 2010, rule 25.18 states that the order should be served on the expert within two days of receipt from the court, so it may be that the order is sent in advance of the letter of instruction. The expert should be asked clarify any areas with the solicitor in the first instance, and if the instruction is in relation to court proceedings the expert can approach the court for clarification if needed, under FPR 2010, rule 25.17.

Experts are always directed to FPR 2010, Part 25 to ensure that they understand their obligations to the court and that they sign the report with the correct statement of truth appended.

It is useful to ensure that the expert understands the timetable for producing the report and responding to any subsequent questions received from either party. The court order will generally indicate how long each party has to raise questions; in default FPR 2010 state that the parties have 10 days from the report being filed to raise written questions.

Likewise, the order will indicate who will be responsible to pay the expert for any additional work done to answer the questions. If the order is silent, then the answers are treated as part of the report and the costs will be shared in the same way that the costs of the report are shared.

Responsibility for payment of the costs of the report should be set out in the order. In default FPR 2010, rule 25.12(6) states that the parties are jointly and severally liable for the payment of the expert's fees and expenses. It is prudent therefore to ensure that the order states that the parties are each responsible for 50% of the costs. This is especially important when one of the parties is a litigant in person.

Annex 4C specifically relates to the instruction of a property expert who needs to know how to access the property and will need to have some paperwork in respect of that property. It may be that there is no need to send the whole lease to the expert, but the expert will need to know the length of the unexpired term of the lease. Practitioners should be sensible when instructing experts, who do not need too much descriptive information about the property as they will be inspecting it themselves.

Annex 4D is a letter of instruction to a pension expert who will need to know whether they are being instructed to calculate income equality in retirement; if so, the expert also needs to know what the date of retirement will be. This can sometimes be a thorny issue for practitioners, particularly if one party does not agree with the age at which the other wishes to retire. This can easily be resolved by both practitioners having a telephone conference with the expert before submitting the letter of instruction rather than inserting multiple dates of retirement as this will produce multiple calculations which will increase the cost of the report. Asking for a number of options to be considered will not always help the practitioner to settle the case as the report will then contain too many permutations.

The expert may be asked to calculate an offsetting figure so that one party can retain equity in the matrimonial home (or other capital) rather than take equality of income through pension transfer. Finally, it may be that the expert is asked to calculate a pension share to ensure a projected income at a certain level at state retirement age.

In the instructions section, the pension expert may also be asked to exclude periods of premarital pension contributions and/or post-separation pension contributions.

When submitting paperwork to the experts it is sensible to also send a signed authority form from each party. This will ensure that the expert can contact the pension trustees directly for any additional information required.

Annex 4E sets out the information required for a single joint expert business/forensic accountant. It should be noted that contact details are provided so that the expert can contact the accountant for the business and other key administrative personnel to obtain the information needed for the report. The expert will also need some background information in respect of the business.

The expert is usually instructed to provide a value of the company and, if each party has a financial interest in the company, to determine the value of the parties' shares. Tax issues are very important, so the expert will need to calculate CGT and any tax relief available if one party were to sell their shares to the other party or back to the business. Finally, the matter of liquidity is very important to understand if the company is to be able to raise the finance to buy out shares or to release capital in the near future.

It may also be important to understand the maintainable future earnings for the party who intends to remain in the business.

When instructed to investigate, a business accountant will sometimes be called a 'forensic accountant' as the accountant is examining evidence.

Annex 4F is a letter to a single joint expert accountant to obtain CGT calculations. In this instance the expert needs to know:

- how much it cost to purchase the asset;
- how much the asset is worth now;
- when dealing with a home, whether this was the primary principal residence (PPR) for either of the parties, giving details of the periods during which that was the case;
- if one of the parties has left the matrimonial home, the date they vacated; if they have not purchased another property, whether they are going to lose their PPR relief and will need to pay CGT;
- any expensive works done to the property that could be deducted from a capital gain before the calculation of tax.

Annex 4G is a letter to the client enclosing the expert's report.

Annex 4A

Letter to the client before the first appointment

Dear [*name of client*]

As you know we are due to attend the Family Court at [*name and address of court*] on [*date and time*]. This is the first hearing of [your] *or* [*name of spouse*]'s application for financial remedy.

As we have exchanged the required paperwork with [*name of spouse*], we now need to prepare for the hearing.

The first hearing

Although your hearing is at [*time*] it is a good idea for you to get there early as you can speak to [me] *or* [your advocate] [your barrister] and discuss your case. Please make sure that you arrive at the Family Court no later than [*time*]. It may be possible to agree a number of matters in advance of seeing the Judge, which would be a good use of the time you have at court.

On the day, a number of cases will all be listed at the same time before the same Judge. This means that you could be at Court [all morning] *or* [all afternoon] *or* [all day]. Please ensure that you make appropriate arrangements to be at Court for this length of time.

You can bring someone to Court to support you if you think this will be helpful. Only the parties and their representatives are allowed into the court room but there is a waiting area for anyone who comes with you. [As your spouse is not represented by a lawyer, [he/she] might make an application for a friend to enter the court room to make notes for [him/her]. [He/she] has not yet made this application but might do so on the day. Your advocate will deal with the application if one is made.]

You will not have to give formal evidence at this hearing. Your advocate will speak to the Judge and the other side for you.

Representation at the hearing

[I propose to represent you at the hearing. I estimate my costs of attending will be [£X], and I will therefore need you to place [£X] on account of costs. This should cover my preparation for the hearing, travel and attendance at the hearing. As you know I charge an hourly rate of [£X] and you will be paying for my time to attend.]

OR

[My colleague [*insert name and status of advocate*] will represent you at the hearing. I estimate [his/her] costs of attending to be [£X], and I will therefore need you to place [£X] on account of costs. This should cover preparation for the hearing, travel and attendance at the hearing. [He/she] charges an hourly rate of [£X] and you will be paying for [his/her] time to attend.]

OR

[I propose to instruct a barrister to attend the hearing to represent you. I will send them the necessary paperwork before the hearing with an outline of the matter. I will also try to speak to them about the case in advance. The barrister I have booked is [*insert name and web profile*]. I am confident that [he/she] will be able to represent you very well on the day. [His/her] costs are fixed at [£X plus VAT]. In addition, [*insert name and status*] will also attend the hearing to assist your barrister. I estimate [his/her] costs to be [£X]. I will therefore need you to pay [£X] on account by no later than [*date*].]

We may be able to settle this case before the hearing which would lead to us asking the Court to cancel the hearing and approve the settlement instead. It is always possible that the Court will experience some difficulty which means that the case is removed from the Court hearing list. This happens from time to time and there is nothing we can do to stop the Court from doing this.

If your case does not go ahead as planned on the [*date*] then you may still have to pay the barrister's fees. I have been told that if we cancel your barrister before [*insert date when the deemed fee becomes due*] then no fee will be payable. If we cancel after this date then the full fee will have to be paid.

If you are being represented by [me] *or* [*name of colleague*] you will only be charged for the actual time we spend on the preparation of your case.

Bundles

[As [you are the applicant in this matter] *or* [your spouse does not have a solicitor in this matter] I need to prepare a bundle of documents for the hearing. This is a straightforward matter at this early stage. I will prepare the paperwork and send it to the court and to the other side once it has been agreed.]

OR

[As [*name of spouse*] is the applicant in this matter, [his/her] solicitor needs to prepare a bundle of documents for the hearing. I will contact them to ensure we get these papers before the hearing, as we have an opportunity to agree the content of the bundle before it is sent to the Judge.]

If you have any questions about the hearing please let me know.

Yours sincerely

Annex 4B
Letter to the client enclosing the FDA order

Dear [*name of client*]

I enclose a copy of the order made by the Judge at the First Appointment hearing on [*date*]. As you know there are a number of things that both you and [*name of spouse*] must do before the next hearing [*insert date of hearing if known*].

Answers to questionnaire

The Judge has said that you must answer [*name of client*]'s questionnaire by no later than [*date*]. I attach a copy of the questionnaire that you must answer; some questions were rejected by the Judge and these have been deleted. Please let me have your answers and documents by [*date*] so that I can prepare the document and send it to you to check and sign.

Valuation expert

The Judge has said that if you can both agree a value of the family home by [*date*] then we can use that value at the next hearing. If not, then we will need to ask an expert to prepare a valuation report.

[*Name of spouse*] has suggested that the value is [£X] and you have said that you think it is [£X]. Are you willing to propose a compromise figure to be used at the next hearing? If so, please let me know and I will propose the figure to the other side.

If not, we will need to find three valuation experts who will be able to prepare report for court purposes. We have used the valuers listed below in the past and I am happy to approach them to see how much they would charge to prepare a valuation report in this case. As you know, the costs of the valuation report would be split equally between you both.

1.
2.
3.

Pension report

The Judge has directed that we obtain a report from a pension expert. We need to propose three pension experts to the other side and the other party can choose one person from these. That person will be appointed as the Court's expert rather than for either of you, and both parties will pay the costs of the report equally.

We need to propose three pension experts by [*date*] and [*name of spouse*] will choose one of the proposed experts. I suggest the three experts listed below, who are all suitably qualified to produce this type of report. I have contacted them to find out if they can prepare a report in the time frame given by the Court. Each expert has confirmed that they are available to prepare the report and they have given me an estimate of their costs based on the information we have.

1. [*Insert name, qualification and costs*].
2. [*Insert name, qualification and costs*].
3. [*Insert name, qualification and costs*].

Please let me know if you are happy for me to propose the above pension experts.

I will need to draft a letter to the pension expert by [*date*]. I will start to draft the letter to send to the other side as [he/she] needs to approve and sign the letter before we send it to the chosen expert.

We shall be allowed to ask further questions when the report is sent out. [*Insert any provision that may have been made on questions to experts.*]

Please let me know if you have any questions regarding these matters.

Yours sincerely

Annex 4C

Letter instructing a property expert

Dear Sirs,

Re: [*Name of applicant*] and [*Name of respondent*]
Family Court sitting at [*location*] – Case No. [*number*]

[You are instructed to prepare a report as a single joint expert in financial proceedings ongoing in the Family Court sitting at [*location*].]

OR

[The parties are in the process of negotiating a settlement and are instructing you to prepare a report to be used in those negotiations. In the event that those negotiations break down it is agreed that your report will be used in financial remedy proceedings, when issued.]

Contact details

Contact name	Status	Address	Telephone number	Mobile number	Email address
[name of applicant]	Applicant				
[applicant's solicitor]	Applicant's solicitor				
[name of respondent]	Respondent				
[respondent's solicitor]	Respondent's solicitor				

Background information

A) [You are instructed pursuant to an order of District Judge [*name*] at the Family Court sitting at [*location*] on [*date*]. [A copy of that order is attached to this letter]/[A copy of that order was sent to you under separate cover as required by FPR 2010, rule 25.18].]

OR

B) [Although there are ongoing divorce proceedings, neither party has issued financial remedy proceedings. Accordingly, you are being instructed to prepare your report to assist the parties [in [mediation]/[the collaborative law process]/[arbitration]] *or* [to negotiate a settlement].]

Your instructions

You are asked to prepare a report providing your opinion on the open market value of the property [*insert address of property*]. You should assume:

1. A willing seller.
2. Sale with vacant possession.
3. That the property is unencumbered at the date of sale.
4. The best price that a willing buyer could reasonably be expected to pay.

If you have any questions in respect of these instructions we would ask that you email the solicitors in the first instance. [You should note that you are entitled to file written requests for directions with the Court: FPR 210, rule 25.17.]

You should send a copy of the report to [the Court and the parties' solicitors]/[the parties' solicitors].

Your report

You are asked to ensure that your report complies with the requirements set out in FPR 2010, Part 25 (**www.justice.gov.uk/courts/procedure-rules/family/parts/part_25**).

1. Rule 25.14 sets out the contents of your report and directs you to have regard to the requirements set out in Practice Direction 25B, specifically para.9.1.
2. The report must be addressed to the Family Court sitting at [*location*] and not to either of the instructing firms or parties.
3. Please ensure that your report is verified by a statement of truth in the following form:

> 'I confirm that I have made clear which facts and matters referred to in this report are within my own knowledge and which are not. Those that are within my own knowledge I confirm to be true. The opinions I have expressed represent my true and complete professional opinions on the matters to which they refer.'

As you are appointed as a single joint expert, it is important to preserve your impartiality. Please ensure that you do not enter into correspondence or have conversations with one party or their adviser without copying the other party, or making a note which should be appended to your report.

Timetable

Your report is due to be filed by [*date*]. If you find that you are unable to file the report with the Court by that date, please contact the Court and both solicitors to inform us of a realistic date when the report will be filed.

For your information the next hearing of this matter is on [*date*]. You are not required to attend to give evidence at the hearing.

The parties are permitted to ask questions about your report, and these questions should be filed within [10] days of the report being filed. We would ask that you answer those questions by [*insert date*].

The cost of answering these questions should be paid for by [the person raising those questions]/[both parties equally].

Access to the property

The property is presently occupied by [*name*]. Please contact [him/her] direct using the contact details above to arrange an appointment to view the property.

[[*Name*] would also wish to be in attendance when the inspection is carried out. Please therefore contact [him/her] using the contact details above.]

OR

[Neither party or their representative should be in attendance when you inspect the property.]

The paperwork

We enclose the following documentation to assist you to prepare your report.

1. A copy of the order dated [*date*].
2. Office copy entries for the property.
3. [A copy of the lease.]

Your fees

A) [Prior to the preparation of your report or carrying out any preliminary work, we should be grateful if you would provide us with an estimate of your costs. Once your fees are agreed, we would ask that you prepare your report.]

OR

B) [You have estimated your fees to be £X, and those fees are accepted by the parties. If there is likely to be an increase in those fees for any reason please contact us before any additional work is undertaken to ensure that those fees are agreed.]

It has been [ordered by the Court] *or* [agreed by the parties] that they will each be responsible for one half of your costs. We would therefore ask that you [invoice both *name of solicitors* and *name of other solicitors*] *or* [prepare an invoice addressed to each party] for one half of your costs.

Yours sincerely

....

[*Name of solicitors*]

Solicitors for [applicant]

Yours sincerely

....

[*Name of solicitors*]

Solicitors for [respondent]

Annex 4D

Letter to pension valuer

Dear Sirs

Re: [*Name of applicant*] and [*Name of respondent*]
Family Court sitting at [*location*] – Case No. [*number*]

[You are instructed to prepare a report as a single joint expert in financial proceedings ongoing in the Family Court sitting at [*location*].]

[The parties are in the process of negotiating a settlement and are instructing you to prepare a report to be used in those negotiations. In the event that those negotiations break down it is agreed that your report will be used in financial remedy proceedings, when issued.]

Background

We act for [*name and date of birth*] in divorce proceedings [*name and date of birth*] is represented by [*name and reference of solicitors*] of [*address and telephone number*].

The parties were married/entered into a civil partnership on [*date*], both parties are in [good] health, [neither party is a smoker]/[our client is a smoker]/[the other party is a smoker].

Contact details

Contact name	Status	Address	Telephone number	Mobile number	Email address
[name of applicant]	Applicant				
[applicant's solicitor]	Applicant's solicitor				
[name of respondent]	Respondent				
[respondent's solicitor]	Respondent's solicitor				

Background information

A) On [date of hearing], the Court ordered that a pension report should be obtained, and [a copy of that order is attached] *or* [a copy of that order was sent to you under separate cover as required by FPR 2010, rule 25.18].

OR

B) [Although there are ongoing divorce proceedings, neither party has issued financial remedy proceedings. Accordingly, you are being instructed to prepare your report to assist the parties [in [mediation]/[the collaborative law process]/ [arbitration]] *or* [to negotiate a settlement].]

Your instructions

It has been [agreed /directed by the Court] that you should be appointed the single joint expert regarding the following matters:

1. To share the pensions accrued to date to create an equality of income at [the parties' respective state retirement age] *or* [the age of 55/60/65].
2. If applicant/respondent wishes to retain [£X] of equity in the family matrimonial home/capital assets how should the pension share in '1' be adjusted to reflect this?
   Detail how the pensions should be shared to produce a projected income for the applicant/respondent at state retirement age of £X,000 per annum in today's terms.
3. Figures are to be considered using pension accrued during marriage only.

If you have any questions in respect of these instructions we would ask that you email the solicitors in the first instance. [You should note that you are entitled to file written requests for directions with the Court: FPR 2010, rule 25.17.]

You should send a copy of the report to [the Court] *and/or* [the parties' solicitors].

The paperwork

We enclose the following:

1. A copy of the order dated [*date*].
2. Details of the pension arrangements for each party, with CE and dates that they were obtained.
3. Extracts from each party's Form E, relating to pensions.
4. Responses to the parties' questionnaires in relation to pensions.
5. Replies to Form P.
6. BR19 state pension forecast.
7. Completed and signed authority forms from each party for each scheme.

Your report

You are asked to ensure that your report complies with the requirements set out in FPR 2010, Part 25 (**www.justice.gov.uk/courts/procedure-rules/family/parts/ part_25**).

1. Rule 25.14 sets out the contents of your report and directs you to have regard to the requirements set out in Practice Direction 25B, specifically para.9.1.
2. The report must be addressed to the Family Court sitting at [*location*] and not to either of the instructing firms or parties.
3. Please ensure that your report is verified by a statement of truth in the following form:

    'I confirm that I have made clear which facts and matters referred to in this report are within my own knowledge and which are not. Those that are within my own knowledge I confirm to be true. The opinions I have expressed represent my true and complete professional opinions on the matters to which they refer.'

As you are appointed as a single joint expert, it is important to preserve your impartiality. Please ensure that you do not enter into correspondence or have conversations with one party or their adviser without copying the other party, or making a note which should be appended to your report.

Timetable

Your report is due to be filed by [*date*]. If you find that you are unable to file the report with the Court by that date, please contact the Court and both solicitors to inform us of a realistic date when the report will be filed.

For your information, the next hearing of this matter is on [*date*]. You are not required to attend to give evidence at the hearing.

The parties are permitted to ask questions about your report. These questions should be filed within [10] days of the report being filed.

We would ask that you answer those questions by [*insert date or days*].

The cost of answering these questions should be paid for by [the person raising those questions] *or* [both parties equally].

Fees

A) [Prior to the preparation of your report or carrying out any preliminary work, please provide us with an estimate of your costs. Once your fees are agreed, please prepare your report.]

OR

B) [You have estimated your fees to be £X, and those fees are accepted by the parties. If there is likely to be an increase in those fees for any reason, please contact us before any additional work is undertaken to ensure that those fees are agreed.]

It has been [ordered by the Court] *or* [agreed by the parties] that they will each be responsible for one half of your costs. We would therefore ask that you [invoice both *name of solicitors* and *name of other solicitors*] *or* [prepare an invoice addressed to each party] for one half of your costs.

Yours sincerely   Yours sincerely

....

[*Name of solicitors*]   [*Name of solicitors*]

Solicitors for [applicant]   Solicitors for [respondent]

Annex 4E
Letter to SJE forensic/business accountant

Dear Sirs,

Re: [*Name of applicant*] and [*Name of respondent*]
Family Court sitting at [*location*] – Case No. [*number*]

[You are instructed to prepare a report as a single joint expert in financial proceedings ongoing in the Family Court sitting at [*location*].]

OR

[The parties are in the process of negotiating a settlement and are instructing you to prepare a report to be used in those negotiations. In the event that those negotiations break down, it is agreed that your report will be used in financial remedy proceedings, when issued.]

Contact details

Contact name	Status	Address	Telephone number	Mobile number	Email address
[name of applicant]	Applicant				
[applicant's solicitor]	Applicant's solicitor				
[name of respondent]	Respondent				
[respondent's solicitor]	Respondent's solicitor				
[name]	Company accountant				
[name]	Company secretary				
[name]	Financial director				

Background information

A) [You are instructed pursuant to an order of District Judge [*name*] at the Family Court sitting at [*location*] on [*date*]. [A copy of that order is attached to this letter] *or* [a copy of that order was sent to you under separate cover as required by FPR 2010, rule 25.18].

OR

B) [Although there are ongoing divorce proceedings, neither party has issued financial remedy proceedings. Accordingly, you are being instructed to prepare your report to assist the parties [in [mediation]/[the collaborative law process]/ [arbitration]] *or* [to negotiate a settlement].]

Background of the business

The business is a [limited company] [partnership] [sole trading business] which was set up by [*name*] on [*date*].

The business specialises in [*insert brief details*].

The applicant [is a [X%] shareholder/director/partner/has no interest in the business] and the respondent [is a [X%] shareholder/director/partner/has no interest in the business].

[*Insert other relevant information about the business.*]

Your instructions

You are asked to prepare a report providing your opinion on:

(a) The value of the company [and the parties' respective interests].
(b) Any taxation issues for the applicant and respondent if they were to sell their shares in the business in the tax year [YY/YY]. Please assume that they both have full CGT allowances.
(c) Please give your opinion on liquidity:

  (i)   How can money be drawn from the business? Please include the tax consequences for each method.
  (ii) What is the maximum sum that can be withdrawn from the business in the next 6–12 months?
  (iii) Can the company raise finance to enable one party to purchase the other's interest?
  (iv) What is the maintainable future income that [*name*] can draw from the business assuming that [*name*] has no further interest in the business?
  (v)   Are there any other issues that need to be addressed that are relevant to the business that should be noted in these proceedings?

If you have any questions in respect of these instructions we would ask that you email the solicitors in the first instance. [You should note that you are entitled to file written requests for directions with the Court: FPR 2010, rule 25.17.]

You should send a copy of the report to [the Court] *and/or* [the parties' solicitors].

Your report

You are asked to ensure that your report complies with the requirements set out in FPR 2010, Part 25 (**www.justice.gov.uk/courts/procedure-rules/family/parts/part_25**).

1. Rule 25.14 sets out the contents of your report and directs you to have regard to the requirements set out in Practice Direction 25B, specifically para.9.1.
2. The report must be addressed to the Family Court sitting at [*location*] and not to either of the instructing firms or parties.
3. Please ensure that your report is verified by a statement of truth in the following form:

   'I confirm that I have made clear which facts and matters referred to in this report are within my own knowledge and which are not. Those that are within my own knowledge I confirm to be true. The opinions I have expressed represent my true and complete professional opinions on the matters to which they refer.'

As you are appointed as a single joint expert, it is important to preserve your impartiality. Please ensure that you do not enter into correspondence or have conversations with one party or their adviser without copying the other party, or making a note which should be appended to your report.

Timetable

Your report is due to be filed by [*date*]. If you find that you are unable to file the report with the Court by that date, please contact the Court and both solicitors to inform us of a realistic date when the report will be filed.

For your information the next hearing of this matter is on [*date*]. You are not required to attend to give evidence at the hearing.

The parties are permitted to ask questions about your report. These questions should be filed within [10] days of the report being filed. We would ask that you answer those questions by [*insert date or days*].

The cost of answering these questions should be paid for by [the person raising those questions] *or* [both parties equally].

The paperwork

We enclose the following documentation to assist you to prepare your report:

1. Form E pages.
2. Business accounts.
3. Evidence to support business valuation.
4. [other].

Further information or documents

If you need any further information you should contact any of the company personnel listed above.

We would ask that you copy the parties' solicitors into any requests for information as you are appointed as the single joint expert in this matter.

Your fees

A) [Prior to the preparation of your report or carrying out any preliminary work, please provide us with an estimate of your costs. Once your fees are agreed, please prepare your report.]

OR

B) [You have estimated your fees to be £X, and those fees are accepted by the parties. If there is likely to be an increase in those fees for any reason, please contact us before any additional work is undertaken to ensure that those fees are agreed.]

It has been [ordered by the Court] *or* [agreed by the parties] that they will each be responsible for one half of your costs. We would therefore ask that you [invoice both *name of solicitors* and *name of other solicitors*] *or* [prepare an invoice addressed to each party] for one half of your costs.

Yours sincerely   Yours sincerely

....

[*Name of solicitors*]   [*Name of solicitors*]

Solicitors for [applicant]   Solicitors for [respondent]

Annex 4F
Letter to SJE accountant to obtain CGT calculations

Dear Sirs,

Re: [*Name of applicant*] and [*Name of respondent*]
Family Court sitting at [*location*] – Case No. [*number*]

[You are instructed to prepare a report as a single joint expert in financial proceedings ongoing in the Family Court sitting at [*location*].]

OR

[The parties are in the process of negotiating a settlement and are instructing you to prepare a report to be used in those negotiations. In the event that those negotiations break down it is agreed that your report will be used in financial remedy proceedings, when issued.]

Contact details

Contact name	Status	Address	Telephone number	Mobile number	Email address
[name of applicant]	Applicant				
[applicant's solicitor]	Applicant's solicitor				
[name of respondent]	Respondent				
[respondent's solicitor]	Respondent's solicitor				

Background information

A) [You are instructed pursuant to an order of District Judge [*name*] at the Family Court sitting at [*location*] on [*date*]. [A copy of that order is attached to this letter] or [a copy of that order was sent to you under separate cover as required by FPR 2010, rule 25.18].]

OR

B) [Although there are ongoing divorce proceedings, neither party has issued financial remedy proceedings. Accordingly, you are being instructed to prepare your report to assist the parties [in [mediation]/[the collaborative law process]/[arbitration]] or [to negotiate a settlement].]

Your instructions

You are asked to prepare a report to calculate the Capital Gains Tax that the [applicant] and/or [respondent] would pay upon the disposal of their interests in the following assets:

1. [*Address of property.*] This property is owned by [*name*] and [*name*] in [*shares*]. The property was purchased on [*date of purchase*] for [*price of purchase*].The current value of the property is [*insert value*]. This was the principal residence of the parties until [*date*] when [*insert address*] became the primary residence.
2. [*Address of property.*] This property is owned by [*name*] and [*name*] in [*shares*]. The property was purchased on [*date of purchase*] for [*price of purchase*]. The current value of the property is [*insert value*]. The [applicant] [respondent] moved out of this property on [*date*]; however, the [respondent] [applicant] remains there and this is [his/her] family home.
3. [*Address of property.*] This property is owned by [*name*] and [*name*] in [*shares*]. The property was purchased on [*date of purchase*] for [*price of purchase*].The current value of the property is [*insert value*].
4. [*Insert details of any improvement works to the property that would reduce CGT.*]

If you have any questions in respect of these instructions we would ask that you email the solicitors in the first instance. [You should note that you are entitled to file written requests for directions with the court: FPR 2010, rule 25.17.]

You should send a copy of the report to [the Court] *and/or* [the parties' solicitors].

Your report

You are asked to ensure that your report complies with the requirements set out in FPR 2010, Part 25 (**www.justice.gov.uk/courts/procedure-rules/family/parts/part_25**).

1. Rule 25.14 sets out the contents of your report and directs you to have regard to the requirements set out in Practice Direction 25B, specifically para.9.1.
2. The report must be addressed to the Family Court sitting at [*location*] and not to either of the instructing firms or parties.
3. Please ensure that your report is verified by a statement of truth in the following form:

    'I confirm that I have made clear which facts and matters referred to in this report are within my own knowledge and which are not. Those that are within my own knowledge I confirm to be true. The opinions I have expressed represent my true and complete professional opinions on the matters to which they refer.'

As you are appointed as a single joint expert, it is important to preserve your impartiality. Please ensure that you do not enter into correspondence or have conversations with one party or their adviser without copying the other party, or making a note which should be appended to your report.

Timetable

Your report is due to be filed by [*date*]. If you find that you are unable to file the report with the Court by that date, please contact the Court and both solicitors to inform us of a realistic date when the report will be filed.

For your information the next hearing of this matter is on [*date*]. You are not required to attend to give evidence at the hearing.

The parties are permitted to ask questions about your report. These questions should be filed within [10] days of the report being filed. We would ask that you answer those questions by [*insert date or days*].

The cost of answering these questions should be paid for by [the person raising those questions] *or* [both parties equally].

The paperwork

We enclose the following documentation to assist you to prepare your report:

1. A copy of the order dated [*date*].
2. Valuation report for property [1/2/3].
3. Office copy entries for property [1/2/3].
4. Completion statements for property [1/2/3].
5. [Invoices for improvement works.]

Your fees

A) [Prior to the preparation of your report or carrying out any preliminary work, please provide us with an estimate of your costs. Once your fees are agreed, please prepare your report.]

OR

B) [You have estimated your fees to be £X, those fees are accepted by the parties. If there is likely to be an increase in those fees for any reason, please contact us before any additional work is undertaken to ensure that those fees are agreed.]

It has been [ordered by the Court] *or* [agreed by the parties] that they will each be responsible for one half of your costs. We would therefore ask that you [invoice both *name of solicitors* and *name of other solicitors*] *or* [prepare an invoice addressed to each party] for one half of your costs.

Yours sincerely   Yours sincerely

....

[*Name of solicitors*]   [*Name of solicitors*]

Solicitors for [applicant]   Solicitors for [respondent]

Annex 4G
Letter to the client enclosing the expert's report

Dear [*name of client*]

I am pleased to inform you that I have received the report of the expert, which I enclose for your attention.

Summary of report

As you can see the expert has indicated that [*summarise the main findings for example the valuation, CGT figure, pension share/offset or business valuation*].

Next steps

You have [10] days within which you can ask the expert to clarify anything in the report. It is therefore important that you read the report straight away so that we can discuss it. If we need to ask questions I will draft these and send them to the expert.

The expert then has [X] days to answer those questions, and this should give us enough time to prepare for the next hearing.

According to the [rules] *or* [order of the Court] the costs of the expert answering the questions will be paid for by [the person asking the questions] *or* [both parties equally].

Fees

You will note that the expert has also sent an invoice for your share of the fees. [These will be discharged using the money held on account] *or* [You need to place £X on account in [7 days] so that we can discharge the invoice].

Yours sincerely

5 Financial dispute resolution

The precedents in this chapter deal with the start of negotiations and matters up to the financial dispute resolution hearing. It is assumed that the other party is represented rather than a litigant in person. If the other party is not represented, the letters to the other side should be adapted to take this into account. It is always worthwhile negotiating with a litigant in person, and the letters to them need to be clear about the terms of any offer and the potential costs of implementing the proposal.

Initially, negotiations are likely to be conducted on a 'without prejudice' basis. There is nothing to stop practitioners from writing 'open' letters to settle early on and this approach is to be commended, as long as the offers are reasonable. Naturally, once an open offer has been made, it is on the table for the court to see.

Financial remedy settlement letters should not be marked 'without prejudice save as to costs' or even worse '*Calderbank* v. *Calderbank*' as these will have no effect on costs in financial remedy proceedings, unless negotiating interim applications such as maintenance pending suit. These references are outdated and should be avoided at all costs.

The costs rules can be found at Part 28 and Practice Direction 28A to FPR 2010. The ordinary rule in financial remedy proceedings is that each party will pay their own costs: FPR 2010, rule 28.3(5). It is possible for a costs order to be made but this is very rare in practice. The provisions that the court must take into account when considering whether or not to make a costs order are at FPR 2010, rule 28.3(7).

5.1 Without prejudice letter to settle

When writing offer letters it is important to pay attention to the way that the parties are referred to in the letter. Sometimes, as in this case, the correspondence is formal, with the parties referred to as 'my client' and 'your client'.

If the practitioners have been on more cordial terms it may be that they have referred to the parties by the first names throughout the correspondence, for example 'Helen would like to remain in the family home with Conor and Lucy until they finish their full-time tertiary education'. There is no need to change the nature of such cordial correspondence when sending a 'without prejudice letter'. The parties will be used to seeing legal letters and as such will not be expecting a sudden change to this more formal style.

It may be that the parties have been referred to as 'Mr and Mrs Singh', which still has a formal feel whilst acknowledging that the parties are not only clients as in the very formal example. It is for individual practitioners to decide which approach they prefer.

When writing to a litigant in person more formal language might be a barrier to settlement. This should be considered before sending the offer letter.

The precedent at **Annex 5A** is a proposed without prejudice letter which is written in a standard format with a brief introduction. The offer is in the main body of the letter and the concluding paragraphs contain a net effect calculation – this is always useful and if the practitioner feels the need to explain a particular aspect of the settlement this is where that explanation would be placed.

It is sensible to send a schedule of assets and income so that there is no confusion as to the precise assets and value of those assets at the time that the offer is made. If no schedule is sent then the letter itself would need to outline the assets. **Annex 3J** has a sample schedule of assets that can be used for this purpose.

It is very helpful for a judge at the financial dispute resolution (FDR) hearing to be able to get an overview of case by reading the initial letters to settle. It is for this reason that details of the parties' ages, length of marriage and children's details are included in the background information. It has long been accepted by the courts that a settled period of cohabitation that leads to marriage should be included when calculating the length of the relationship for MCA 1973, s.25(2)(d).

In the body of the letter, neutral terminology is used to put forward a proposal which should always include relevant time limits, costs and undertakings if required. In this precedent, it is proposed that a jointly owned home is transferred from joint names into the wife's sole name although she is unable to release the husband from his mortgage covenants. It is not unusual in average case negotiations for one party to want to transfer the property without being able to release the other from the mortgage. At the minimum, the mortgage company will probably need to give consent to transfer the property even if the mortgage is not transferred. In the alternative, the property could remain in the parties' joint names in which case the beneficial ownership would be declared in the order (this is known as a 'Mesher' order).

In this case, the wife has agreed to pay the monthly mortgage payments, other outgoings and has agreed to indemnify the husband against any breach of the mortgage covenants. She has also agreed to give an undertaking to use her best endeavours to release him from the mortgage as soon as possible. In **Annex 5B** the implications of the offer are explained to him as the undertaking is difficult to enforce and the indemnity would only be used after the mortgage company has recouped arrears from him. He would then enforce the indemnity against the wife but this would only be fruitful if she had assets against which he could enforce. It is possible that this could be effected against her share of the equity in the family home.

It is important to note that the offer should be clear about the way that net equity is calculated, and this is set out clearly at para.5. Occasionally, practitioners negotiate on a 'net equity' figure but when it comes to drafting the order they convert that into a gross equity calculation. This should be avoided at all costs. The practitioner should not switch from net to gross equity figures as this affects the sum that the recipient will receive.

Example

Value of property – £300,000

Mortgage redemption (today's figure) £123,456

Costs of sale (2.5%) £7,500

Total equity = £169,044

35% = £59,165.40

If switching to use the gross equity figure for 35%, take the cash sum due to the recipient – £59,165 and represent it as against the value of the property which is £300,000. This means that the recipient is entitled to 19.72% of the gross value of the property.

If the husband gets his share when the property is worth £400,000 in five years' time, under the net calculation he would receive:

Property value – £400,000

Mortgage – £123,456

Costs of sale (2.5%) – £10,000

Net equity = £266,544

35% = £93,290.40

Using the gross calculation in five years' time against a property worth £400,000:

Property value – £400,000

19.72% = £78,880

That is a loss to the recipient of **£14,410.40,** just by converting the net sum into a gross figure.

Paragraph 6 sets out the events upon which the husband can expect to receive his money. These are often referred to as 'trigger events', and all of these events are subject to negotiation. Many courts do not allow a trigger event that is referable to one party's cohabitation. Cohabitation can be a difficult matter to prove and it requires the parties to have a high degree of interaction with each other after the divorce which can be intrusive and unwanted.

As the property is being secured as a home for the benefit of the children, it is unusual for the husband's charge to be paid to him while the children are still minors. Paragraph 7 makes it very clear that even if one of the trigger events occurs, the husband will not receive his money if the children are still minors and in full-time education or training.

It appears that the parties have agreed that the husband will pay school fees and reasonable extras. It is sensible to set out what those extras will be or how they will be agreed in the future. The husband is to pay the fees for the children's current schools or any schools that they may attend in future by mutual agreement.

The wife would like spousal maintenance to be paid at a fixed rate of £1,000 per calendar month subject to an annual variation referable to Consumer Price Index (CPI) increases. In the alternative, she could ask for annual variation referable to Retail Price Index (RPI) increases or a fixed percentage increase, which is much more unusual to see in financial remedy orders.

It is important to state whether the wife will be entitled to apply for an extension of the maintenance term. If it is not intended that she will be able to extend the term, a s.28(1A) MCA 1973 bar should be imposed and specifically referred to in the offer letter. Paragraph 11 makes it clear that she will be allowed to apply for an extension.

The responsibility to pay the costs of any pension sharing implementation should be in the offer. If this is overlooked then the costs will be the responsibility of the transferor in their entirety.

The matter of contents and personal belongings should always be addressed. If the parties have not already divided these, they will need to draw up lists of those items that they want to keep and these would form part of the negotiations.

Paragraphs 15 and 16 deal with the clean break provisions. The wife cannot have a clean break on income until her maintenance term has expired. She is therefore entitled to make an application during that time under the Inheritance (Provision for Family and Dependants) Act 1975.

The client proposes that each party will pay their own costs, and this is in line with the general costs provision for financial remedy cases. However, it appears that a costs order was made in respect of the divorce proceedings and it was agreed that the husband would pay costs at the rate of £1,500. Although this is part of the divorce proceedings, it is possible to use this as a negotiating matter in the financial remedy proceedings.

It is usual for there to be liberty to apply in respect of timing and implementation.

5.2 Letter to the other side advising on the without prejudice offer

This letter is sent with reference to the offer made in the letter at **Annex 5A**. When sending an offer to settle to the client, it is quite important to present it in either neutral or positive terms. If it is a first offer which is not one which the client would be likely to accept, it should be presented to the client with suggestions of possible areas where it might be possible to negotiate a better settlement. It may even be a good idea to meet with the client before giving them a copy of the letter – in that way the terms of the offer can be discussed with the client, hopefully avoiding the client reacting badly to the contents of the letter.

If the practitioner can explain to the client why the offer is made in potentially unfavourable terms, this is an important message for the client to hear. In this case, the offer is made on the basis that the wife and children will remain in the family home. If the practitioner knows that the client wants the family home to be sold this should be addressed when presenting the offer letter to the client.

If clients have unreasonable expectations of the settlement, they should be informed of the most likely outcomes. This is a delicate line to tread: on the one hand, the practitioner does not want to allow the client hold unreasonable expectations but, on the other hand, the client is entitled to give instructions to settle; that may not immediately accord with the way the court would deal with things. Practitioners hope that those initial, unreasonable views will change. This is most likely to happen when the clients have been to the FDR hearing and heard the judge's views on the likely settlement prospects.

The FDR hearing is designed so that the judge conducting the hearing can assess both parties' settlement proposals and help the parties to narrow the areas of dispute. There is a good prospect that the parties will be able to reach a final agreement at the FDR hearing or very soon after the hearing with the help of the judge.

5.3 Letter to the client before the financial dispute resolution hearing

The letter to the client before the financial dispute resolution hearing at **Annex 5C** mirrors the earlier precedent at **Annex 4A** informing the client about the impending hearing, the costs of attendance and the options for representation. In this letter the client is informed that the client will be expected to negotiate a settlement of the financial matters at the FDR hearing.

It is usual to warn the client about the increased costs between the FDR hearing and the final hearing. These costs usually double, at the very least. It is important that the client accounts for the potential costs when considering whether to accept a proposed offer or when making a counter offer at the hearing.

The practitioner should bear in mind the importance of instructing counsel at an early stage and possibly having a conference with counsel before the FDR hearing.

The Family Justice Council has produced some very good best practice guidance regarding FDR hearings which should be taken into account. This guidance can be found at **www.judiciary.gov.uk/wp-content/uploads/2014/10/fjc_financial_ dispute_resolution.pdf**.

5.4 Conclusion

FDR hearings are fraught with tension for clients, who will have spent several months embroiled in court proceedings and spent thousands of pounds on legal representation. Clients usually want to reach a settlement at this hearing but need to be reassured that they are making the right decisions. If the fee earner with conduct of the case is not able to represent the client, it is a good idea for them to be in attendance at the hearing with counsel or available at the end of the telephone if the client wants to discuss a proposed settlement.

Clients always feel under pressure to settle and there is always the possibility that the client complains after a successful FDR hearing. Client should never be forced to enter into an agreement unless they are certain that that is what they want to do.

Annex 5A

Without prejudice letter to settle

Without Prejudice

Dear Sirs

We write to you in the hope that the parties may be able to reach a settlement of these matters without the necessity to attend the next hearing on [*date*].

Background

Our client is [*insert age*] years old and works on a full-time basis as a [*insert occupation*]. She is claiming tax credits and child benefit, and she is therefore maximising her earning capacity. Your client is [*insert age*] years old and also works on a full-time basis as a [*insert occupation*]. He too is maximising his earning capacity. The parties have been in a settled relationship of 15 years, including 5 years of premarital cohabitation.

The attached schedule of assets and income shows the parties' respective positions. It is clear that there is a substantive disparity between their net income positions.

The children are [*insert name of child and age*] and [*insert name of child and age*]. Both live with their mother at the family home and have substantive contact with their father.

Both parties have agreed that they would like the children to continue to attend their current schools, and this will therefore mean that money will need to be found to pay their school fees.

Our offer

Our client has instructed us to propose the following, on the basis that the children remain in the family home which is nearby to their schools.

1. The jointly owned family home be transferred to our client, subject to the current mortgage. The transfer shall take place within 28 days of the sealed consent order being received by the parties.
2. Our client is not in a position to release your client from his covenants under the mortgage. However, she is willing to take over the payments for the mortgage immediately. In addition, she is willing to offer an indemnity to your client in respect of the mortgage obligations.
3. She will also give him an undertaking to use her best endeavours to release him from the mortgage as soon as possible.
4. Your client will register a charge against the property upon completion of the transfer; this will be to secure his share of the net equity at 35%.

5. The net equity of the property will be calculated as the value of the property minus the mortgage at the date of the agreement. This currently stands at [*insert redemption figure*], less the costs of sale fixed at 2.5%.

6. Your client can expect to be paid the monies secured by way of charge, upon the occurrence of the first event listed below:

    a.   the youngest child of the family finishing his full-time secondary education or attaining the age of 18 years (whichever is the later);

    b.   the death of the applicant;

    c.   the applicant remarrying or cohabiting with another person as husband-and-wife for a continuous period of more than 12 months;

    d.   the applicant's failure to occupy the property for a period of 3 months in any 12-month period;

    e.   the applicant's failure to occupy the property as her primary residence;

    f.   further order.

7. The events that trigger the payment of your client's money shall not be exercisable without permission of the court while any child of the family in occupation of the property is still a minor or of full age but receiving full-time education or training.

8. Your client will pay all school fees and reasonable extras as appearing on the school bill. These shall be paid as and when demanded by the school. This obligation shall be in respect of both children for the schools they currently attend or any school that the parties agree the children should attend in the future.

9. Your client will pay child maintenance at the figure assessed by the Child Maintenance Service.

10. Your client will pay spousal maintenance for our client at the rate of £1,000 per calendar month. Such maintenance will be paid until the occurrence of the first of the following events:

    a.   the youngest child of the family finishing full-time secondary education or attaining the age of 18, whichever is the later;

    b.   the death of the applicant or respondent;

    c.   the applicant cohabiting with another person as husband-and-wife for a continuous period of more than 12 months;

    d.   further order.

11. The applicant may apply for an order to extend this term.

12. The spousal maintenance payments shall be varied annually in line with any increase of the Consumer Price Index (CPI).

13. There shall be a 42% pension sharing order in favour of the applicant. The parties will pay the costs of the trustees for pension sharing implementation equally. This is in line with pension expert's report.

14. The parties have divided the contents of the family home between them. If there are any personal items that your client wishes to take he should provide a list of these for our client's consideration.

15. There shall be a clean break in respect of your client's claims against ours in life and death.

16. There shall be a clean break in respect of our client's claims, save for her income claims which will remain open until expiration of the term. When our client's maintenance comes to an end she will no longer be able to make an application under the Inheritance (Provision for Family and Dependants) Act 1975, s.2.
17. Each party shall pay their own costs in respect of the financial remedy proceedings. There is a costs order that your client is to pay the costs of divorce. We agreed to cap these costs at £1,500. The costs should be paid within 14 days of the Decree Absolute being pronounced.
18. There shall be liberty to apply.

Net effect

The above offer is designed to minimise any disruption to the children, which the parties both agree is their goal. Our client will remain in the family home and we accept that until she is able to release your client from his covenants under the joint mortgage, he is unlikely to be able to purchase another property. He is currently living in rented accommodation and although he would like to purchase a property this is not likely to be possible until he receives his share of the net equity in the family home.

Your client will receive net equity of 35%. The small departure away from equality is to reflect the money that he withdrew from the parties' joint savings account when he left the family home. This money was used to pay the deposit at the property he currently rents and the first month's rent. He will receive the deposit money back when he vacates the property. Save for that one small adjustment, the above offer reflects an equal division of the property and pensions.

You will note from the attached schedule of assets that your client will be left with 40% of his net income, after he has paid the school fees and child and spousal maintenance as per the terms of the order. His net income will allow him to pay his rent and reasonable costs of living as per his outgoings schedule.

We believe that the above offer is fair to both the parties as they will both continue to maintain a standard of living which is similar to that enjoyed by them during the marriage. Our client understands that your client wants to purchase a property rather than rent a property; sadly, the current circumstances do not allow for this.

We should be grateful if you could take your client's instructions and revert to us within 21 days with his response.

Yours faithfully

Annex 5B

Letter to the other side advising on the without prejudice offer

Dear [*name of client*]

I am pleased to inform you that we have received an offer to settle from [*name of spouse*]. This is only a first offer but I recommend that we start to think about putting together a counter offer if you decide that you do not want to accept this offer.

The offer

The attached offer proposes that [*name of spouse*] and the children remain in the family home. I know that you would ideally like the home sold so that you are released from the mortgage but [*name of spouse*] would like to remain living there with the children. She has offered to pay the monthly mortgage instalments and all the outgoings but as you know, she is unable to release you from the mortgage as she doesn't earn enough.

She has offered you an indemnity. This means that if she fails to pay the mortgage she would protect you from any losses you incur if the mortgage company pursue you for the arrears. This will not prevent the mortgage company from making you pay arrears, but it does mean that you could get those back from her, if she has the money to pay you. At this stage we do not know whether the mortgage company will consent to transfer the property from your joint names into her sole name. She will need to make some enquiries about this issue before you can seriously consider her offer.

Housing needs

I appreciate that this is not the offer you had hoped for; however, this is the only way that she could stay in the family home with the children, which is what she wants. The family home is a three bed semi-detached property so she is not living in a property that is too big for her.

I know that you believe that she could move to a different area and buy a smaller three bed terraced house which would allow her to release you from this mortgage. A judge may not agree that your proposal is sensible or fair. We can hear from the Judge at the FDR hearing what he/she thinks about it. In the meantime, we can discuss putting this forward as a counter proposal.

Equity

She is offering you 35% of the net equity in the property, which would be calculated by using the value of the property at the time you were to get your money. The current redemption figure for the mortgage would be deducted, and this means that you would not benefit from any mortgage payments that reduce the sum outstanding to the mortgage company. [*Name of spouse*] should not be able to increase the capital sum outstanding to the mortgage company. In my view, fixing the redemption figure to the current value is fair.

The costs of sale fixed at 2.5% would also be deducted; this is usual although we may be able to negotiate the figure down to 2%. I have prepared an example of the calculation below, based on the value of the property at £300,000.

Worked example

Value of property – £300,000

Mortgage redemption (today's figure) – £123,456

Costs of sale (2.5%) – £7,500

Total equity = £169,044

35% = £59,165.40

Although she indicates that she is offering you an equal share in the property, she has adjusted the division of equity to take into account the money that you withdrew from the joint savings account, by agreement, when you left the house. I understand that you used this money for the first month's rent, six weeks' deposit and some furniture for the property that you are renting, which you will keep. You have previously informed me that you are likely to lose some of the deposit as the children have damaged a doorway with their toys and crayons. Obviously this is a matter that we need to discuss further.

Pension

She has offered to settle with a pension share in line with the expert's report. I think this is reasonable under the circumstances. She is offering to share the costs of implementation equally.

Maintenance

She has indicated that she wants you to pay her spousal maintenance of £1,000 per calendar month. This is in additional to child maintenance at the CMS rate. I know that you were hoping that you would not need to pay [*name of spouse*] spousal maintenance if she agreed to sell the family home and downsize to a smaller property. If you look at the schedule of assets and income, you can see that you can afford to pay the sum of £1,000 pcm if you reduce your expenditure. She has not offered to reduce her expenditure, which is not extravagant but could be trimmed in places.

School fees

She says that you have both agreed that the children should continue at their private fee-paying schools and that you will pay the school fees and reasonable extras. Please let me know whether you have agreed this.

Costs

She has proposed that you will each pay your own legal costs in respect of the financial negotiations but would like you to pay the agreed sum of £1,500 in respect of the divorce costs. An order was made that you pay these costs but we may be able to negotiate this when we prepare a counter offer.

I would ask you to consider the terms of the overall offer and let me know if you would like to accept this offer or whether you would like me to put together a counter offer. It is a good idea to put together an offer as soon as possible as we may be able to settle matters before the next hearing.

I look forward to hearing from you.

Yours sincerely

Annex 5C

Letter to the client before the financial dispute resolution hearing

Dear [*name of client*]

As you know, we are due to attend the Family Court at [*insert name and address of court*] on [*insert date and time*]. This is the financial dispute resolution (FDR) hearing of [your] *or* [*name of spouse*]'s application for financial remedy.

We have now exchanged offers to settle with [*name of spouse*], so we should have some useful negotiations at this hearing.

The FDR hearing

Although your hearing is at [*time*] it is a good idea for you to get there early as you can speak to [me] *or* [your advocate] [your barrister] and discuss your case. Please make sure that you arrive at the Family Court no later than [*time*]. We have been asked to attend the hearing at least one hour in advance of the hearing time so that we can negotiate with [*name of spouse*]'s advocate.

The court will expect you to be ready to negotiate a settlement of these matters on the day, [your representative] will advise you on any offers that [*name of spouse*] makes and whether to accept or make any counter offers. You must consider all offers that are made and seriously consider whether you want to settle or continue with the litigation. The next hearing will be the final hearing. Your costs will at least double between this hearing and the final hearing and you should bear this in mind when you are negotiating at the FDR hearing.

On the day, a number of cases will all be listed at the same time before the same Judge. This means that you could be at court [all morning] *or* [all afternoon] *or* [all day]. Please ensure that you make appropriate arrangements to be at Court for this length of time.

You can bring someone to Court to support you if you think this will be helpful. Only the parties and their representatives are allowed into the court room but there is a waiting area for anyone who comes with you. [As your spouse is not represented by a lawyer, [he/she] might make an application for a friend to enter the court room to make notes for them. [He/she] has not yet made this application but might do so on the day. Your advocate will deal with the application if one is made.]

You will not have to give formal evidence at this hearing. Your advocate will speak to the Judge and the other side for you.

Representation at the hearing

[I propose to represent you at the hearing. I estimate my costs of attending will be [£X], and I will therefore need you to place [£X] on account of costs. This should cover my preparation for the hearing, travel and attendance at the hearing. As you know I charge an hourly rate of [£X] and you will be paying for my time to attend.]

OR

[My colleague [*insert name and status*] will represent you at the hearing. I estimate [his/her] costs of attending to be [£X], and I will therefore need you to place [£X] on account of costs. This should cover preparation for the hearing, travel and attendance at the hearing. [He/she] charges an hourly rate of [£X] and you will be paying for [his/her] time to attend.]

OR

[I propose to instruct a barrister to attend the hearing to represent you. I will send them the necessary paperwork before the hearing with an outline of the matter. I will also try to speak to them about the case in advance. The barrister I have booked is [*insert name and web profile*] [who represented you at the first hearing]. I am confident that [he/she] will be able to represent you very well on the day. [His/her] costs are fixed at [£X plus VAT]. In addition, [*insert name and status*] will also attend the hearing to assist your barrister, and I estimate [his/her] costs to be [£X]. I will therefore need you to pay [£X] on account by no later than [*date*].

It is possible that we will be able to settle this case before the hearing which would lead to us asking the Court to cancel the hearing and approve the settlement instead. It is possible that the Court will experience some difficulty which means that the case will be removed from the Court hearing list. This happens from time to time and there is nothing we can do to stop the Court from doing this.

If your case does not go ahead as planned on [*date*] then you may still have to pay the barrister's fees. I have been told that if we cancel your barrister before [*insert date when the deemed fee becomes due*] then no fee will be payable. If we cancel after this date then the full fee will have to be paid.

If you are being represented by [me] *or* [*name of colleague*] you will only be charged for the actual time we spend on the preparation of your case.

Bundles

[As [you are the applicant in this matter] *or* [your spouse is the applicant but does not have a solicitor in this matter], I need to prepare a bundle of documents for the hearing. This is a straightforward matter at this early stage. I will prepare the paperwork and send it to the court and to the other side once it has been agreed.]

OR

[As [*name of spouse*] is the applicant in this matter, [his/her] solicitor needs to prepare a bundle of documents for the hearing. I will contact them to ensure we get these papers before the hearing, as we have an opportunity to agree the content of the bundle before it is sent to the Judge.]

If you have any questions about the hearing please let me know.

Yours sincerely

6 Final hearing

6.1 Introduction

The precedents in this section deal with preparation up to the final hearing. Most of the work will already have been done but the applicant will need to prepare the trial bundle for the final hearing, and if the applicant is a litigant in person, the first represented respondent will prepare the trial bundle index. It is good practice to provide a copy of the trial bundle to the litigant in person, who should be consulted about the content of the trial bundle. **Annex 6A** deals with the trial bundle index which accords with Practice Direction 27A to FPR 2010. The summary, statement of issues, chronology and reading list should all be agreed where possible and should be a single document.

Unless the court has directed otherwise, the bundle should be no more than 350 pages. For this reason it is sensible to file the Forms E without the attachments unless they are going to be referred to in the hearing,

Both parties should be trying to reach a settlement of matters. If an agreement is reached then a consent order should be drafted and submitted to the court, which is dealt with in **Chapter 7**.

6.2 After the FDR hearing

The letter at **Annex 6B** outlines those matters that will have been dealt with at the FDR hearing if an agreement is not reached. The court will usually want the parties to file statements, sometimes referred to as 'section 25 statements'. The statement will stand as the evidence in chief for each client, although further brief oral evidence is usually permitted. The evidence contained within the statement should refer to MCA 1973, s.25.

The court may order updated property valuations and direct both parties to file updated disclosure. This is either done separately to filing the statement or can sometimes be dealt with within the statement.

The court will require the parties to file updated housing particulars to show appropriate housing for themselves and for the other party. It is imperative that the client produces good quality property particulars, preferably in colour so that the judge has a good idea of the properties that are proposed. Clients should also visit the proposed properties, particularly if they are proposing that property as their children's main housing. They are likely to be cross-examined about the housing particulars especially if the issue of alternative housing is central to the financial remedy case.

6.3 Statement

Annex 6C sets out the bare bones of a section 25 statement, structured around the s.25(2) factors (a)–(h) in MCA 1973. Those factors form subheadings with the relevant information included underneath. Each paragraph should be numbered sequentially, each page should be numbered and only information that has not previously been referred to should be included. The practitioner should note that this is not a position statement, it is a witness statement which should accord with the requirements at Practice Direction 22A.

The Practice Direction sets out a lot of detail about the preparation of a witness statement. It specifies that where dates and figures are expressed, numbers should be used. Where documents are mentioned these should be noted in the margin or in bold text.

Where exhibits are attached to the statement the first page of each exhibit should be marked in the same way as the first page of the witness statement, noting the details on the top right hand corner of the statement. Occasionally the court will limit the number of pages that the parties may submit in the statements and those limits should be strictly observed.

6.4 Open position

The letter at **Annex 6D** follows the outline of the without prejudice letter at **Annex 5A**. The notable difference is that this letter is not marked 'without prejudice'.

In the first paragraph of the letter, it is noted that this is the open proposal to be used at the final hearing. The applicant must file this 14 days in advance of the hearing: FPR 2010, rule 9.28. This letter is much more formal than the without prejudice offer as this will be presented to the court at the final hearing. It would be more usual for the parties to be referred to as 'your client'/'my client' or 'Mr and Mrs X' rather than 'David and Helen' in this letter.

The practitioner should consider how to adapt this letter if it is being sent to a litigant in person.

The open position should be a realistic offer to settle matters, as the court will take this as a starting point.

The main difference between this letter and the without prejudice letter is that the terms are different, and the terms in this offer are likely to be less advantageous. This means that if there is a without prejudice offer on the table at the same time, it is likely to offer more favourable terms than the open position.

The asset schedule is said to show the net effect position of the offer, which is of great practical assistance to the judge.

The offer now proposes a net equity share of 45% at para.4 but the trigger events at para.6 are now different. The wife is only offering to release the husband's interest when the youngest child finishes full-time tertiary education, to include a gap year. This means that the husband will get his money much later than under the terms of the without prejudice offer, even though he is being offered a larger share.

The wife no longer intends to release his interest if she starts to cohabit, even though this was previously offered on a without prejudice basis.

The wife now proposes that the husband pays both school and university fees at para.8; previously she was content with only school fees being paid.

The wife is now seeking a higher rate of spousal maintenance per calendar month; this is increased by £200 per calendar month and ends when the youngest child finishes full-time tertiary (not secondary) education to include a gap year, or remarriage or the death of either party. Previously, she was willing to accept the termination of her maintenance in the event that she cohabited for a significant period of time.

The net effect reasoning is much the same. It does not refer to the increased time to pay spousal maintenance or receive the net equity in the home. These matters are always subject to negotiation and the court has a wide discretion whether to include these or not.

Respondents are required to submit their open position seven days after receiving the applicant's open position.

6.5 Costs estimate

Form H1 Statement of Costs (financial remedy) is the costs schedule that must be filed prior to the final hearing. This should be filed not less than 14 days before the final hearing: FPR 2010, rule 9.27(2). It is available at **formfinder.hmctsformfinder. justice.gov.uk/form-h1-eng.pdf.**

Practitioners sometimes overlook this as the Form H only needs to be filed at a hearing and not in advance of it. Form H1 needs to be served on the other party as well as being filed with the court. The format of the Form H1 is similar to that of the Form H, and the first page contains a 'summary of costs' statement.

Section A: this information can be copied over from the Form Hs filed previously as long as those estimates were accurate. It is worth looking over the time recording and bills to ensure that the estimates given previously can be used at this stage.

Section B: all post-issue costs up to and including the FDR appointment should be included. This is a composite of information provided in the first and second Form H filed at the FDA and FDR hearing.

Section C: this is new information about the costs incurred after the FDR hearing and up to the date that the form is signed (14 days before the final hearing).

Section D: this is an estimate of costs incurred after the date the form is signed and up to the end of the final hearing.

Section E: this is an estimate of costs of implementation. This estimate should be thought through properly if there are property transfers and pension implementation costs. The costs of implementation can sometimes be quite high and are not always accurately estimated.

If the practitioner intends to seek a costs order to be made against the other party, the Form N260 should be filed, available online at **formfinder.hmctsformfinder. justice.gov.uk/n260-eng.pdf.**

6.6 Conclusion

The case should be administratively ready for a final hearing. Counsel will need to be instructed in advance of the hearing and having a conference with counsel is very important. Negotiations will continue to the door of the court in the hope that the parties will be able to reach an agreement rather than having an order imposed upon them.

Annex 6A

Trial bundle index

IN THE FAMILY COURT AT [*location*]

CASE No:

IN THE MATTER OF THE MATRIMONIAL CAUSES ACT 1973
BETWEEN:

<table>
<tr><td align="center">[Name of applicant]</td><td align="right">Applicant</td></tr>
<tr><td align="center">– and –</td><td></td></tr>
<tr><td align="center">[Name of respondent]</td><td align="right">Respondent</td></tr>
</table>

Index to trial bundle for final hearing

[*Insert date and time*]

[*Insert name of judge*]

A	Date	Preliminary Documents	Page
		Summary of the background of the case	
		Statement of issues to be determined	
		Applicant's Position Statement	
		Respondent's Position Statement	
		Chronology	
		Skeleton argument (applicant)	
		Skeleton argument (respondent)	
		List of essential reading	
B		**Application and Orders**	
		FDA order	
		FDR order	
		Directions order	

C		Statements	
		Applicant's Form E (no attachments)	
		Respondent's Form E (no attachments)	
		Applicant's replies to Respondent's questionnaire	
		Respondent's replies to Applicant's questionnaire (no attachments)	
		Applicant's first statement (no attachments)	
		Respondent's first statement (no attachments)	
		Applicant's second statement with exhibits	
		Husband second statement with exhibits	
D		Property Expert's report	
		SJE report	
		SJE updating valuation	
		Questions to the expert	
		SJE's response to questions	
		Pension Expert's report	
		SJE report	
		Questions to expert	
		SJE's response to questions with additional calculations	
E		Housing particulars and mortgage capacity	
		Applicant's mortgage capacity	
		Respondent's mortgage capacity	
		Applicant's proposed housing particulars for respondent	
		Applicant's proposed housing particulars for self	

Annex 6B
Letter to the client sending the FDR order

Dear [*name of client*]

I enclose a copy of the order made by the Judge at the FDR hearing on [*date*]. Unfortunately you were unable to reach an agreement with [*name of spouse*] on the day. We can continue to negotiate in the hope that we do not need to go to the final hearing.

In the meantime, we must ensure that we deal with those matters that the Judge ordered at the FDR hearing, just in case we do not settle these matters.

Statements

Both of you have been ordered to file statements before the next hearing to summarise your positions. I will start to prepare the statement which needs to address the legal points that the Judge will take into account when making a decision about the division of finances. Please note that this is not an opportunity to say whatever you like about [*name of spouse*], since the statement needs to deal with a number of specific matters.

Your statements must be exchanged on [*date*], I propose to send you a first draft of the statement by no later than [*date*] and you should be ready to send me an amended version of the statement by [*date*]. I would therefore hope to be able to file the statement on time and exchange it with [*name of spouse*].

Updated disclosure

The Judge wants you both to update your financial disclosure by [*date*]. This means that you need to provide updated bank statements, credit card statements, payslips, P60, business accounts and any other financial information to ensure that we have a complete picture of your financial circumstances. Much of this information will be used to produce an up-to-date schedule of assets before the final hearing.

The Judge will only see those documents that are very important at the final hearing. He or she does not need to see every document produced in the disclosure process.

Updated housing particulars and mortgage capacity

It is important that we have a good idea of the cost of housing for both you and [*name of spouse*]. For this reason, the Judge has indicated that you should produce updated housing information by [*date*]. Please make sure I have these details by no later than [*date*].

As I have informed you previously, it is a good idea to produce full colour estate agents' particulars rather than print black and white property details from a website. The Judge will be given copies of these housing particulars.

I would also encourage you to visit the properties that you are proposing for yourself and for [*name of spouse*]. You are likely to be asked questions at the final hearing about these properties and so it is vital that you have done more than just obtain details from a website.

Although you have already produced a document which shows your mortgage capacity, if your overall income position has changed for the better or worse then you should produce a current mortgage capacity document.

Updated valuation

The Judge has given us permission to approach the single joint expert property valuer to provide us with an updated property valuation. [*Name of spouse*]'s solicitor and I will arrange for this updated report to be made available by no later than [*date*].

We do not need an updated pension expert's report. The Judge did not give us permission to update the report, which has only just been produced in any event.

We do not yet know the date of the final hearing, and as soon as I know the date I will contact you with it.

Yours sincerely

Annex 6C
Outline section 25 statement

Case no.:

IN THE FAMILY COURT SITTING AT [*location*]

Name of deponent:

Number of statement:

Exhibits:

Date of statement:

BETWEEN:

[Name of applicant]   Applicant

– and –

[Name of respondent]   Respondent

Witness statement of [*name*]

I [*insert name and address*] make this statement pursuant to an order of [*name of judge*] made on [*date*].

1. The income, earning capacity, property and other financial resources which each of the parties to the marriage has or is likely to have in the foreseeable future, including in the case of earning capacity any increase in that capacity which it would in the opinion of the court be reasonable to expect a party to the marriage to take steps to acquire.

    a. [*refer to current income and benefits/tax credits and ability to increase income*]

2. The financial needs, obligations and responsibilities which each of the parties to the marriage has or is likely to have in the foreseeable future.

    a. [*refer to housing particulars and the condition of the proposed housing by other side*]
    b. [*refer to mortgage capacity and ability to repay the mortgage if relevant*]

3. The standard of living enjoyed by the family before the breakdown of the marriage.

    a. [*insert brief details to expand on information given in the Form E*]

4. The age of each party to the marriage and the duration of the marriage.

    a.   *[detail any period of cohabitation before the marriage]*
    b.   *[if relevant, set out the date of separation and if there is any dispute expand on the information previously given]*

5. Any physical or mental disability of either of the parties to the marriage.

    a.   *[update on any conditions mentioned in the Form E or any new conditions, attach evidence]*

6. The contributions which each of the parties has made or is likely in the foreseeable future to make to the welfare of the family, including any contribution by looking after the home or caring for the family.

    a.   *[this is probably already covered in the Form E and other statements; if this refers to future contributions then include it here]*

7. The conduct of each of the parties, if that conduct is such that it would in the opinion of the court be inequitable to disregard it.

    a.   *[litigation misconduct can be mentioned here]*
    b.   *[if the other party has spent wantonly during the proceedings this can be mentioned here – subject to taking advice]*

8. In the case of proceedings for divorce or nullity of marriage, the value to each of the parties to the marriage of any benefit ... which, by reason of the dissolution or annulment of the marriage, that party will lose the chance of acquiring.

    a.   *[mention any other matters that might be relevant]*

9. Other circumstances.

    a.   *[the court is obliged to take into account any other matters that might be relevant, and these should be included here]*

I believe that the facts stated in this witness statement are true.

....

Signed

Dated

Annex 6D

Open position

Dear Sirs

We write to you with our client's open proposal prior to the final hearing on [*date*]. We look forward to receiving your client's open position in 7 days.

Background

Our client is [*age*] years old and works on a full-time basis as a [*occupation*]. She is claiming tax credits and child benefit, and she is therefore maximising her earning capacity. Your client is [*age*] years old and also works on a full-time basis as a [*occupation*]. He too is maximising his earning capacity. The parties have been in a settled relationship of 15 years, including 5 years of premarital cohabitation.

The attached schedule of assets and income shows the parties' respective positions. It is clear that there is a substantive disparity between their net income positions. That schedule also shows the net effect of our open proposal.

The children are [*insert name of child and age*] and [*insert name of child and age*]. Both live with their mother at the family home and have substantive contact with their father.

Both parties have agreed that they would like the children to continue to attend their current schools. This will therefore mean that money will need to be found to pay their school fees.

Our offer

Our client has instructed us to propose the following, on the basis that the children remain in the family home which is near to their schools.

1. The jointly owned family home be transferred to our client, subject to the current mortgage. The transfer shall take place within 28 days of the sealed consent order being received by the parties.
2. Our client is not in a position to release your client from his covenants under the mortgage. However, she is willing to take over the payments for the mortgage immediately. In addition, she is willing to offer an indemnity to your client in respect of the mortgage obligations.
3. She will also give him an undertaking to use her best endeavours to release him from the mortgage as soon as possible.
4. Your client will register a charge against the property upon completion of the transfer; this will be to secure his share of the net equity at 45%.

5. The net equity of the property will be calculated as the value of the property minus the mortgage at the date of the agreement. This currently stands at [*insert redemption figure*], less the costs of sale fixed at 2.5%.

6. Your client can expect to be paid the monies secured by way of charge, upon the occurrence of the first event listed below:

   a. the youngest child of the family finishing his full-time tertiary education up to the end of the first degree, to include a gap year;
   b. the death of the applicant;
   c. the applicant remarrying;
   d. further order.

7. The events that trigger the payment of your client's money shall not be exercisable without permission of the court while any child of the family in occupation of the property is still a minor, or of full age but receiving full-time tertiary education or training.

8. Your client will pay all school or university fees and reasonable extras as appearing on the school or university bill. These shall be paid as and when demanded by the school or university. This obligation shall be in respect of both children for the schools they currently attend or any school that the parties agree the children should attend in the future.

9. Your client will pay child maintenance at the figure assessed by the Child Maintenance Service.

10. Your client will pay spousal maintenance for our client at the rate of £1,200 per calendar month. Such maintenance will be paid until the occurrence of the first of the following events:

    a. the youngest child of the family finishing full-time tertiary education up to the end of the first degree to include a gap year;
    b. remarriage of the applicant;
    c. the death of the applicant or respondent.

11. The applicant may apply for an order to extend this term.

12. The spousal maintenance payments shall be varied annually in line with any increase of the Consumer Price Index (CPI).

13. There shall be a 42% pension sharing order in favour of the applicant, and the parties will pay the costs of the trustees for pension sharing implementation equally. This is in line with the pension expert's report.

14. The parties have divided the contents of the family home between them.

15. There shall be a clean break in respect of your client's claims against ours in life and death.

16. There shall be a clean break in respect of our client's claims, save for her income claims which will remain open until expiration of the term. When our client's maintenance comes to an end, she will no longer be able to make an application under the Inheritance (Provision for Family and Dependants) Act 1975, s.2.

17. Each party shall pay their own costs in respect of the financial remedy proceedings. There is a costs order that your client is to pay the costs of divorce. We agreed to cap these costs at £1,500. The costs should be paid within 14 days of the Decree Absolute being pronounced.

18. There shall be liberty to apply.

Net effect

The above offer is designed to minimise any disruption to the children, which the parties both agree is their goal. Our client will remain in the family home and we accept that until she is able to release your client from his covenants under the joint mortgage, he is unlikely to be able to purchase another property. He is currently living in rented accommodation, and although he would like to purchase a property this is not likely to be possible until he receives his share of the net equity in the family home.

Your client will receive net equity of 45%. The small departure away from equality is to reflect the money that he withdrew from the parties' joint savings account when he left the family home. This money was used to pay the deposit at the property he currently rents and the first month's rent. He will receive most of the deposit money back when he vacates the property. Save for that one small adjustment, the above offer reflects an equal division of the property and pensions.

You will note from the attached schedule of assets that your client will be left with 30% of his net income after he has paid the school fees and child and spousal maintenance as per the terms of the order. His net income will allow him to pay his rent and reasonable costs of living as per his outgoings schedule.

We believe that the above offer is fair to both the parties as they will both continue to maintain a standard of living which is similar to that enjoyed by them during the marriage. Our client understands that your client wants to purchase a property rather than rent a property; sadly, the current circumstances do not allow for this.

We look forward to receiving a copy of your client's open position.

Yours faithfully

7 Draft orders

7.1 Introduction

This chapter deals with the orders that family practitioners will be asked to draft during the financial remedy process. In recent years, there has been a move by the President of the Family Division to standardise all orders in the Family Court. As a result of these efforts, there are many standard template orders available at **www. judiciary.gov.uk/publications/report-of-the-financial-remedies-working-group-31-july-2014**.

Although it is not mandatory to use these templates they are widely used across England and Wales by practitioners and the judiciary. For many years, practitioners have used the Resolution precedents for consent orders, but these have been broadly replaced by the standard orders referred to above. The precedents shown in this section are based on the standard orders, which means that the orders all have the same foundations.

7.2 First directions appointment

Annex 7A is a fairly typical FDA order that sets out those matters that the parties must deal with before they are able to start to negotiate a settlement.

The parties are to be defined at the start of the order; it is recorded that the applicant has attended a MIAM but that the respondent has not. The respondent has given an undertaking to attend a MIAM before the next hearing. The respondent will therefore be asked to sign the warning in the box that sets out the consequences of failing to comply with an undertaking. As the applicant has not given an undertaking there is no need for them to sign the warning box. Practitioners should note that it is rare for a respondent to be directed to attend a MIAM or to give an undertaking to attend after proceedings have commenced.

In the orders section, the parties have been directed to send to the court and serve on the other party their replies to questionnaires as amended. The practitioner should note that the court sometimes does not require replies to questionnaires to be sent to the court. Although the order does not specify that the replies should be signed with the statement of truth, this is a requirement of FPR 2010.

The parties are required to serve property particulars on the other side, limited to five each. Clients are therefore required to obtain good quality property details that would give the judge at the FDR hearing and the other side a good indication of the type of property and geographical location in which clients propose to house themselves and their ex-spouse and children.

Each party is required to provide evidence of their mortgage raising capacity. This clause specifies that a mortgage broker should be approached to obtain this information. It can sometimes be unhelpful if parties obtain information about their mortgage raising capacity by using an online tool as this is unlikely to be accurate. If the parties only approach the current lender (without approaching other lenders), it is not likely to be an accurate portrayal of their mortgage raising capacity. In order to get a full picture, the parties should be transparent about the information they give the mortgage broker and the options they are given for borrowing money. Ideally, they should go to an independent mortgage adviser and not a tied broker who would only be able to give them an indication of the amount that could be borrowed from their sources.

The parties are both directed to update disclosure. This can either be by a specified date and time or a set number of weeks before the next hearing. Paragraph 6 is a standard clause and covers all of the information that the parties are likely to need to update, so there is no doubt regarding what is needed.

Paragraph 7 deals with the value of the matrimonial home which can either be agreed by the parties or in default of an agreement a single joint expert can be appointed. It is specified that a chartered surveyor will be appointed; occasionally an estate agent is appointed as estate agents' costs are likely to be lower but usually they provide a less accurate valuation. Estate agents should not provide a market value for the property as this is unhelpful – the court needs to know the sale value for the property.

At para.8 the pension provider is directed to complete the Form P. This form is sometimes used to obtain additional information in respect of the pension; see **formfinder.hmctsformfinder.justice.gov.uk/form-p-eng.pdf**.

Some courts direct the completion of this form more often than others; FPR 2010, rule 9.15(7)(c) indicates that the court has power to direct a party to file and serve information required on a Pension Inquiry Form, otherwise known as the Form P.

A pension expert is appointed at para.9 and it can be seen that some of the information needed in the letter of instruction is set out at (a) and (b). It is much more helpful for some information regarding the instruction to be contained within the body of the order, rather than no information at all. This information will help parties to draft the letter of instruction (**Annex 4D**).

The matter is directed to be listed for an FDR appointment, and the parties are instructed to attend in advance for the purpose of negotiation. This order requires the applicant to prepare a bundle in compliance with Practice Direction 27A.

Paragraph 13 states that the applicant should send a schedule of without prejudice and open proposals prior to the FDR appointment. If this provision is not specified in the order the practitioner should note that there is a requirement under FPR 2010, rule 9.17(3) to file the offers seven days before the FDR hearing.

This order indicates that there is no order for costs; however, it is more usual for the court to make an order that costs are 'in the application', which leaves open the possibility that the court could make a costs order against either party at a later date. Although this is not likely to happen in most cases, the judiciary tend not to make an order that is a 'no order for costs' order but prefer to keep the options open.

7.3 FDR order

Annex 7B represents a typical FDR order where the parties have not been able to reach a settlement of matters. If the parties had reached a settlement, they could file a 'heads of agreement' document at court, which sets out the main terms of agreement between the parties. In this case the matter would be listed for a 'mention' hearing for 10 minutes at a fixed date in the future, to ensure that the parties file the consent order.

Ideally, the parties would draft and submit a consent order while at court, but for many reasons this is not always possible.

As no undertakings are given, the warning box has been removed.

The parties have been directed to file replies to schedules of deficiencies. It is sometimes the case that the parties do not accept that the original questionnaires have been properly answered. This would prompt them to prepare a document called the 'schedule of deficiencies'. This document follows the format of the questionnaire and indicates which questions the other party has failed to answer in full or which documents have not been produced.

Occasionally supplemental questions are raised as a result of answers given to the original questionnaire. The rules require the parties to seek the court's permission to raise supplemental questions or to provide answers to them: FPR 2010, rule 9.16.

The parties are directed to file concise narrative statements dealing with the s.25 factors. See **Annex 6C** for a template statement.

The parties are directed to file updated housing particulars and mortgage capacity documents. This is a good opportunity for the parties to ensure that the housing particulars are up to date for the final hearing.

Appropriate housing for the children of the family is usually central to any financial remedy case. It is vital that this information is as accurate as possible. It may be that there is no need to change the mortgage raising information but if there has been any change in the parties' income, this will be an opportunity to update the mortgage information.

The parties are highly likely to be cross-examined about the mortgage raising documentation and the housing particulars they have submitted. If clients have submitted details of properties, practitioners should always advise clients to visit those properties prior to the final hearing. This is so that they can give comprehensive evidence about the properties that they have proposed. Clients should also visit the properties proposed by the other party so that their evidence is not based on the paper particulars alone.

The parties are also directed to file updating disclosure in a similar way to the first appointment order. The updating disclosure is not likely to form part of the trial bundle at the final hearing but is needed to ensure that the schedule of assets is accurate and that full and frank disclosure is given in a controlled and costs proportionate way throughout the proceedings.

It is vital that the valuation of real property is accurate and so permission is given to update any valuation that was directed after the FDA. The SJE evidence is likely to be six months out of date by the time the final hearing is listed and if the property market is volatile, the expert's initial report will be dated.

The matter is directed to be listed for a further hearing and the applicant is directed to prepare the bundle in accordance with Practice Direction 27A.

7.4 Consent order

The order at **Annex 7C** is the final order as it represents the financial settlement reached by the parties. This order would be sent in duplicate to the court together with Form D81 and the appropriate application form: FPR 2010, rule 9.26. A filing fee will need to be paid.

If the consent order is prepared at court following a successful FDR hearing, no D81 needs to be filed (FPR 2010, rule 9.26(5)) and no filing fee needs to be paid.

If the consent order is submitted following a successful arbitration, the parties should also send a copy of the arbitrator's award with the above documentation. This is to ensure that the judge is aware of the arbitration proceedings. The President of the Family Division has endorsed the use of arbitration (see **www.familyarbitrator. com/wp-content/uploads/Arbitration-in-the-Family-Court-arbitration_pguidance_ nov_15.pdf**).

The order is in a familiar format, following that of the standard order precedents. There is more information in the recitals section. It is clear that this order deals with all financial claims between the parties. This consent order identifies the real property, mortgage and defines the net proceeds of sale at para.4.

The order states that neither party has any legal or equitable interest in the property or assets owned by the other, save for any orders made for the distribution of assets. This ensures that each party can retain those assets they have in their sole name without the need to specify every asset in the body of the order.

The contents of the family home are stated to remain with the party who has them, but it is important to confirm with the client that this is correct. Once the order is sealed by the court it will be too late for either party to ask for the return of items held by the other party.

At para.9, the respondent who will receive maintenance confirms that if her husband predeceases her, any claim she has under his estate will be limited to a sum to compensate her for her lost maintenance.

7.5 Orders

Under the words 'it is ordered', there is intended to be a sale of the family home, followed by payment of specified costs and charges, before the entire net proceeds of sale is paid to the respondent.

The respondent agrees to discharge the mortgage and utilities payments. She also agrees to indemnify the applicant against any liability.

The applicant will pay the respondent maintenance, initially as interim maintenance and then when the Decree Absolute is pronounced substantive maintenance at the rate of £400 per month, reducing to £250 per month when the family home is sold. The practitioner should always draft maintenance provisions carefully to ensure that interim maintenance is followed by substantive maintenance after the Decree Absolute.

The maintenance order is subject to a term and will cease when one party dies, the respondent remarries or cohabits with another man for a period of six months, or at a specified date in the future. Once her maintenance terminates, the respondent is no longer permitted to make any further financial provision applications.

Paragraph 13 ensures that it is clear that the respondent is not allowed to make an application to extend the term maintenance as there is a s.28(1A) MCA 1973 bar.

The respondent's claims for lump sum property adjustment orders and pension sharing orders are dismissed at para.14.

All of the applicant's claims against the respondent are dismissed at para.15. Many courts require both parties to make financial claims against the other before allowing those claims to be dismissed.

The order confirms that there shall be no order for costs, meaning that each party will pay their own costs in respect of the financial matters.

Finally para.17 confirms that each party shall have liberty to apply if issues arise in relation to the implementation and timing of the terms of the order. This does not mean that the parties can re-open the financial matters, but it does mean that they can return to court if there are issues relating to implementation that need to be looked at again.

7.6 Conclusion

Final orders, whether made by consent or otherwise, can be very tricky to draft as there will be many assets that need to be taken into account. If the practitioner drafts a well-worded offer letter (see **Annex 5A** or **6D**) it should be easy to draft an order. An up-to-date schedule of assets can also be invaluable to ensure that all of the assets are dealt with in the offers and in the order.

Annex 7A

FDA order

IN THE FAMILY COURT AT [*location*]

CASE No:

The Matrimonial Causes Act 1973

The marriage of [*name*] and [*name*]

After hearing [*name the advocate(s) who appeared*]

After consideration of the documents lodged by the parties

ORDER MADE BY [*NAME OF JUDGE*] ON [*DATE*] SITTING IN PRIVATE AT A FIRST DIRECTIONS APPOINTMENT

WARNING: IF YOU DO NOT COMPLY WITH THIS ORDER, YOU MAY BE HELD TO BE IN CONTEMPT OF COURT AND YOU MAY BE SENT TO PRISON, BE FINED, OR HAVE YOUR ASSETS SEIZED.

The parties

1. The applicant is [*name of applicant*]

   The respondent is [*name of respondent*]

Recital as to a MIAM

2. It is recorded that the applicant has attended a MIAM
3. The respondent undertakes to attend a MIAM before the next hearing of this matter

---

You may be held to be in contempt of court and imprisoned or fined, or your assets may be seized, if you break the promises that you have given to the court.

If you fail to pay any sum of money which you have promised the court that you will pay, a person entitled to enforce the undertaking may apply to the court for an order. You may be sent to prison if it is proved that you –

a. have, or have had since the date of your undertaking, the means to pay the sum; and

b. have refused or neglected, or are refusing or neglecting, to pay that sum.

I understand the undertakings that I have given, and that if I break any of my promises to the court I may be sent to prison for contempt of court.

....

[*Name*]

Orders

IT IS ORDERED THAT:

4. Both parties shall send to the court and serve on the other party their respective replies to the other's questionnaire and request for further documents as amended by the judge by [*time and date*].

5.

   a. Each party shall serve on the other party copy particulars of properties they consider to be suitable to meet their own and the children of the family's housing needs, and the housing needs of the other party and the children of the family (limited to 5 of each) by [*time and date*].

   b. Each party shall serve on the other party evidence of their mortgage raising capacity by [*time and date*], such evidence to be in the form of a certificate from a mortgage broker, indicating (i) the maximum mortgage that the broker believes he/she will be able to secure and (ii) the repayments that would be required on that mortgage on a repayment basis and on an interest only basis.

   c. Each party shall have permission to serve on the other party such evidence upon which they seek to rely in relation to the other's mortgage capacity within [*number*] days of receipt of the other's evidence as to their own mortgage capacity.

6. Each party shall serve on the other party their updating disclosure by [*time and date*]. Updating disclosure means the disclosure of the following documents:

   a. copies of all bank and building society statements relating to accounts in the category required by paragraph 2.3 of Form E, covering the period from the last statement which has been disclosed to the date of updating disclosure, or covering the period from the opening of the account to the date of updating disclosure for any such accounts which have come into existence since Form E;

   b. a copy of the most up-to-date statement or dividend counterfoil relating to investments in the category required by paragraph 2.4 of Form E, including in respect of any investments which have come into existence since Form E;

   c. a copy of an up-to-date surrender value for policies in the category required by paragraph 2.5 of Form E, including in respect of any policies which have come into existence since Form E;

   d. copies of documents evidencing the up-to-date amount due on liabilities in the category required by paragraph 2.9 or 2.10 of Form E, including in respect of any liabilities which have come into existence since Form E;

   e. copies of any business accounts which have become available since Form E for businesses in the category required by paragraph 2.11 of Form E, including in respect of any businesses which have come into existence since Form E, identifying the expected share of business profits from these accounts;

   f. copies of an up-to-date statement showing the cash equivalent of any pension rights (or value of any PPF rights) in the category required by paragraph 2.13 of Form E, including in respect of any pension rights or PPF rights which have come into existence since Form E;

g. copies of all P60s and P11Ds received since Form E, and all payslips received since the last P60;

h. copies of all tax returns sent to HMRC and tax assessments since Form E; and

i. copies of all documents evidencing all income received since Form E in the nature of dividends, interest, rental income, state benefits or otherwise.

7. The value of the property at [*insert address of matrimonial home*] be agreed if possible. In default of agreement by [*time and date*], the parties shall jointly instruct a chartered surveyor to act as a single joint expert and to provide a valuation report in respect of the property at [*insert address of matrimonial home*] and the following consequential provisions shall apply:

a. The parties shall agree the identity of the single joint expert by [*time and date*]. If the parties cannot agree the identity of the single joint expert, the applicant shall provide the respondent with a list of three appropriate experts by [*time and date*], and the respondent shall select an expert from the list by [*time and date*].

b. The letter of instruction shall be drafted by the [*applicant*] and agreed with the [*respondent*] by [*time and date*] or determined by the court in default of agreement.

c. The letter of instruction and [*insert any other documents*] shall be sent to the expert by [*time and date*].

d. The report shall be sent to the court (in both hardcopy and electronic format) and served on the parties simultaneously by [*time and date*].

e. The costs charged by the expert for preparing the report shall be met by the parties equally in the first instance.

f. Any questions shall be put to the expert by no later than 10 days after receipt of the report (in accordance with FPR 2010, rule 25.10).

g. The expert shall respond to those questions by [*time and date*].

h. The costs charged by the expert for answering those questions shall be met by the parties equally in the first instance.

8. The applicant should obtain from their pension provider to send to the court and serve on the parties a copy of the completed Form P (pension inquiry form)] by [time and date].

9. The parties shall jointly instruct a pensions expert to act as a single joint expert and to provide a report, addressing the following matters:

a. the most cost-effective way to divide the pension provision available to both parties between the parties so as to provide equality of pension income when the applicant reaches their state pension age;

b. an estimate of the pension income that would be receivable by the applicant/ respondent in each of the scenarios in paragraph a above;

and the following consequential provisions shall apply:

c. The applicant shall provide the respondent with a list of three appropriate experts by [*time and date*].

d. The respondent shall select one of the experts from the list by [*time and date*].

e. The letter of instruction shall be drafted by the applicant and agreed with the respondent by [*time and date*], or determined by the court in default of agreement.

f. The letter of instruction and [*insert any other documents*] shall be sent to the expert by [*time and date*].

g. The report shall be sent to the court (in both hardcopy and electronic form) and served on the parties simultaneously by [*time and date*].

h. The costs charged by the expert for preparing the report shall be met by the parties equally in the first instance.

i. Any questions shall be put to the expert by no later than 10 days after receipt of the report (in accordance with FPR 2010, rule 25.10).

j. The expert shall respond to those questions by [*time and date*].

k. The costs charged by the expert for answering those questions shall be met by the parties equally.

10. Save as is expressly ordered by the court, no further expert evidence shall be admissible before the court.

11. The application shall be listed for a financial dispute resolution appointment before a [*name or level of judge*] at the Family Court sitting at [*location*] on the first open day after [*date*] with a time estimate of [*hours/days*]. The parties and their legal advisers shall attend the court building at least one hour prior to the listing time of the financial dispute resolution appointment to negotiate and attempt to narrow the issues.

12. The applicant shall prepare a bundle complying with Practice Direction 27A to FPR 2010.

13. The applicant shall send to the court a schedule of the without prejudice and open proposals made by each party for the resolution of the matters in dispute not later than [*number*] days before the financial dispute resolution appointment].

14. No order as to costs.

Dated

Approved by [*name*]

Annex 7B

FDR order

IN THE FAMILY COURT AT [*location*]

CASE No:

The Matrimonial Causes Act 1973

The marriage of [*name*] and [*name*]

After hearing [*name the advocate(s) who appeared*]

After consideration of the documents lodged by the parties

ORDER MADE BY [*NAME OF JUDGE*] ON [*DATE*] SITTING IN [PRIVATE] AT A FINANCIAL DISPUTE RESOLUTION APPOINTMENT

> **WARNING: IF YOU DO NOT COMPLY WITH THIS ORDER, YOU MAY BE HELD TO BE IN CONTEMPT OF COURT AND YOU MAY BE SENT TO PRISON, BE FINED, OR HAVE YOUR ASSETS SEIZED.**

The parties

1. The applicant is [*name of applicant*]
   The respondent is [*name of respondent*]

IT IS ORDERED (BY CONSENT) THAT:

Replies to schedule of deficiencies and supplemental questionnaire

2. Both parties shall send to the court and serve on the other party their respective replies to the other's schedule of deficiencies and supplemental questionnaire and request for further documents by [*time and date*].

Concise narrative statements

3. Both parties shall send to the court and serve on the other party a concise narrative statement dealing with all of the relevant factors listed in section 25 of the Matrimonial Causes Act 1973 by [*time and date*].

Evidence regarding mortgage raising capacity and housing needs

4.
   a.   Each party shall serve on the other party copy particulars of properties they consider to be suitable to meet their own and the children of the family's housing needs, and the housing needs of the other party and the children of the family (limited to 5 of each) by [*time and date*].

   b.   Each party shall serve on the other party evidence of their or the other party's mortgage raising capacity by [*time and date*], such evidence to be in the form of a certificate from a mortgage broker, indicating (i) the maximum mortgage that the broker believes he/she will be able to secure and (ii) the repayments that would be required on that mortgage on a repayment basis and on an interest only basis.

Updating disclosure

5.   Each party shall serve on the other party their updating disclosure by [*time and date*]. Updating disclosure means the disclosure of the following documents:

   a.   copies of all bank and building society statements relating to accounts in the category required by paragraph 2.3 of Form E, covering the period from the last statement which has been disclosed to the date of updating disclosure, or covering the period from the opening of the account to the date of updating disclosure for any such accounts which have come into existence since Form E;

   b.   a copy of the most up-to-date statement or dividend counterfoil relating to investments in the category required by paragraph 2.4 of Form E, including in respect of any investments which have come into existence since Form E;

   c.   a copy of an up-to-date surrender value for policies in the category required by paragraph 2.5 of Form E, including in respect of any policies which have come into existence since Form E;

   d.   copies of documents evidencing the up-to-date amount due on liabilities in the category required by paragraph 2.9 or 2.10 of Form E, including in respect of any liabilities which have come into existence since Form E;

   e.   copies of any business accounts which have become available since Form E for businesses in the category required by paragraph 2.11 of Form E, including in respect of any businesses which have come into existence since Form E, identifying the expected share of business profits from these accounts;

   f.   copies of an up-to-date statement showing the cash equivalent of any pension rights (or value of any PPF rights) in the category required by paragraph 2.13 of Form E, including in respect of any pension rights or PPF rights which have come into existence since Form E;

   g.   copies of all P60s and P11Ds received since Form E, and all payslips received since the last P60;

    h.   copies of all tax returns sent to HMRC and tax assessments received since Form E; and

    i.   copies of all documents evidencing all income received since Form E in the nature of dividends, interest, rental income, state benefits or otherwise.

Updating property valuations for final hearing

6. In relation to any real property valued prior to the financial dispute resolution appointment and in relation to which either party wishes to assert that the value has significantly changed since that valuation was undertaken the parties shall instruct (by way of an agreed joint letter of instruction) the single joint expert to express a view on whether there has been any change in value since the initial report and, if so, what is the current value. The costs of this exercise shall be met by the parties equally in the first instance.

Further hearing(s)

7.

    a.   The application shall be further listed as follows:

        for a final hearing before [*name or level of judge*] on [*time and date*] (time estimate: [*days/hours*]).

    b.   Both parties shall attend the final hearing to give oral evidence.

    c.   A bundle will be prepared in accordance with Practice Direction 27A. The bundle must be agreed, if possible, by both parties, but the applicant shall take the lead in preparing the bundle. The bundle must be paginated and the documents shall be in chronological order within each section. The bundle must be lodged at court by not later than [*number*] days before the final hearing.

    d.   The bundle should, if possible, include an agreed schedule of assets and liabilities. Where the schedule cannot be agreed then the bundle should include the schedule of assets contended for by each party which should identify which items are not agreed between the parties.

Costs

9. No order as to costs.

Dated:

Approved by: [*name*]

Annex 7C

Consent order

IN THE FAMILY COURT AT [*location*]

CASE No:

The Matrimonial Causes Act 1973

The marriage of [*name*] and [*name*]

After hearing [*name the advocate(s) who appeared*]

After consideration of the documents lodged by the parties

ORDER MADE BY [*NAME OF JUDGE*] ON [*DATE*] SITTING IN PRIVATE

> **WARNING: IF YOU DO NOT COMPLY WITH THIS ORDER, YOU MAY BE HELD TO BE IN CONTEMPT OF COURT AND YOU MAY BE SENT TO PRISON, BE FINED, OR HAVE YOUR ASSETS SEIZED.**

The parties

1. The applicant is [*name of applicant*]

   The respondent is [*name of respondent*]

Definitions

2. The 'family home' shall mean [*insert address*], registered at HM Land Registry.
3. 'The mortgage' shall mean the mortgage secured upon the family home in favour of [*insert lender's details*].
4. 'The net proceeds of sale' shall mean the actual sale price of the property concerned (including any sum paid for fixtures and fittings) less the amount outstanding on the mortgage, the solicitors' conveyancing costs, estate agents' costs and any other costs in connection with the sale which have been agreed by the parties.

Recitals

5. The parties agree that the terms set out in this order are accepted in full and final satisfaction of:
   a. all claims for income;
   b. all claims for capital, that is payments of lump sums, transfers of property and variations of settlements;
   c. all claims in respect of each other's pensions;

    d.   all claims in respect of the contents of the family home and personal belongings including but not limited to furniture, art work, jewellery and motor vehicles;

    e.   all claims in respect of legal costs including those of the divorce proceedings;

    f.   all claims against each other's estate on death;

    g.   all other claims of any nature which one may have against the other as a result of their marriage howsoever arising either in England and Wales or in any other jurisdiction.

6. The parties agree that neither of them has any legal or equitable interest in the property or assets owned by the other, and neither of them has any liability for the debts of the other, except as provided for in this order.

7. The parties agree that neither of them shall institute proceedings against the other under the Married Women's Property Act 1882/the Law of Property Act 1925/the Trusts of Land and Appointment of Trustees Act 1996.

8. The parties agree that the contents of the family home shall remain the absolute property of the person in whose possession they now are.

9. The respondent acknowledges that, if the applicant predeceases her, any claim that she may make against the applicant's estate under the Inheritance (Provision for Family and Dependants) Act 1975 shall be limited to seeking a sum to compensate them for the loss of the periodical payments the applicant was ordered to pay them at paragraph [*insert*] below for themselves.

IT IS ORDERED (BY CONSENT) (WITH EFFECT FROM DECREE ABSOLUTE):

10. The family home shall be sold forthwith on the open market for sale and the following conditions will apply:

    a.   the property shall be placed on the open market for sale immediately by the respondent for such price as may be agreed between the parties or in default of agreement determined by the court;

    b.   the property shall be sold for such price as may be agreed between the parties or in default of agreement as determined by the court;

    c.   both parties shall have conduct of the sale;

    d.   both parties will nominate solicitors for conduct of the conveyancing work;

    e.   such estate agents as may be agreed between the parties or in default of agreement determined by the court shall offer the property for sale; and

    f.   the proceeds of sale shall be applied as follows:

        i.   to discharge the mortgage;

        ii.   in payment of the solicitors' conveyancing costs and disbursements in connection with the sale;

        iii.   in payment of the estate agents' charges;

        iv.   in payment of the balance to the respondent.

11. The respondent shall discharge as and when each payment becomes due, be solely responsible for and in any event indemnify the applicant against:

a. all interest and capital repayments due in respect of the mortgage;

b. all sums due in respect of council tax, utilities (including but not limited to gas, electricity, water and telephone accounts); and

c. buildings and contents insurance premiums in respect of the family home.

The payments shall start on the date of this order and shall end on the sale of the family home.

12. The applicant shall pay to the respondent maintenance pending suit until the date of Decree Absolute and afterwards periodical payments. From the date of this order until the first to occur of the completion of the sale of the family home or [date] the payments shall be at the rate of £400 per month; thereafter the rate of periodical payments shall be varied automatically to the rate of £250 per month. The payments shall be payable monthly in advance by standing order. Payments shall start on [date].

The payments shall end on the first to occur of:

a. the death of either the applicant or the respondent;

b. the respondent's remarriage or cohabitation with another man for a period of 6 months or periods which together amount to 6 months;

c. [date]; or

d. further order;

after which the respondent's claims for periodical payments and secured periodical payments shall be dismissed, and it is directed that upon the expiry of the term, the respondent shall not be entitled to make any further application in relation to the marriage for an order under the Matrimonial Causes Act 1973, s.23(1)(a) or (b) for periodical payments or secured periodical payments.

13. Pursuant to the Matrimonial Causes Act 1973, s.28(1A), the respondent may not apply for an order to extend this term.

14. Except as provided for in this order, the respondent's claims for lump sum orders, property adjustment orders, pension sharing orders and pension attachment orders shall be dismissed.

15. Except as provided for in this order, the applicant's claims for periodical payments orders, secured periodical payments orders, lump sum orders, property adjustment orders, pension sharing orders and pension attachment orders shall be dismissed, and he shall not be entitled to make any further application in relation to the marriage for an order under the Matrimonial Causes Act 1973, s.23(1)(a) or (b) and he shall not be entitled on the respondent's death to apply for an order under the Inheritance (Provision for Family and Dependants) Act 1975, s.2.

16. There shall be no order as to costs.

17. The parties shall have liberty to apply to the court concerning the implementation and timing of the terms of this order only.

Dated:

....

Applicant

....

Respondent

8 Schedule 1 Children Act proceedings

8.1 Introduction

This chapter deals with those cases where the parties are not married but there are claims that can be made in respect of the children of the family.

An application can be made to the Family Court for periodical payments for the children, a lump sum order in respect of children's expenses, or the transfer or settlement of property for the benefit of the children.

These applications are usually made between unmarried parents but can be made in respect of a step-parent who was married or in a civil partnership.

An application for periodical payments can also be made by a guardian or special guardian or any person named in a child arrangements order with whom the child is to live.

The court has jurisdiction even if the child lives outside the jurisdiction of England and Wales, as long as one parent lives within the jurisdiction.

8.2 Informing the client about the applications

The letter at **Annex 8A** explains to the client the claims that can be made for the benefit of the child. It is assumed that the letter is written to the mother with whom the child resides. As the claims are for the benefit of the child, one parent will be the payer and that person will not make cross-applications.

Whilst there is no requirement for the parties to enter into a consent order upon reaching an agreement, it is sensible to record any terms in the form of an order and send it to the court for approval in the usual way. As these matters are governed by the Children Act 1989 and not MCA 1973, the court will be more likely to approve any agreements reached by the parties.

The letter explains the mother's right to make applications for maintenance in certain circumstances. Subparagraphs A–E should be carefully selected to ensure that the court has jurisdiction to make maintenance orders instead of or in addition to the CMS.

The Child Support Act 1991 sets out those circumstances where the CMS does not have jurisdiction to make a maintenance assessment:

(a) due to a child's age;

(b) if one of the parents is outside the jurisdiction;

(c) where an application for educational expenses is to be paid;

(d) where an application for expenses related to a disability is to be paid;

(e) where the maximum assessment has been made, the court will have jurisdiction to make a 'top up' order;

(f) where maintenance is sought from a step-parent.

The practitioner should ensure that claims can be made before sending the letter to the client, or at least couch the letter in more general terms if the client is unaware of the other parent's financial circumstances.

8.3 Making the application

Form A1 'Notice of [intention to proceed with] an application for a financial remedy (other than a financial order)' is online at **formfinder.hmctsformfinder. justice.gov.uk/form-a1-eng.pdf**. The form is in a familiar format as it is similar to the Form A at **Annex 2A**.

The application is much more straightforward as there are fewer claims that can be made by the applicant. The applicant must insert the full names of the parties and indicate which applications for financial orders they propose to make. These must be thought through much more carefully than in MCA 1973 applications as some claims may not be relevant; for example, the applicant may not be able to claim maintenance from the court if the CMS has made an assessment which is not a maximum assessment, unless that application is withdrawn.

If the application form is being sent with a consent order it should be attached to the form and submitted with the necessary paperwork and fee.

On the second page the applicant must indicate whether the applicant is entitled to make a claim for child maintenance from the court. These matters are dealt with above. Usually, step-parents would be asked to pay maintenance within a financial order application (Form A), an application for financial remedy to be resolved following the breakdown of the marriage or civil partnership. However, if those claims were not dealt with at that time, step-parents may face an application under the Children Act 1989 for maintenance in respect of children of the family.

The application form specifically refers to the jurisdiction of the court to make periodical payments orders and requires the applicant to indicate whether the child support agency (CMS) has made a maintenance calculation.

The applicant is required to give details for the children and state where they reside if it is outside England and Wales. This is to establish whether the court has jurisdiction to make the orders requested.

Details of service are straightforward, as are the pages in respect of the MIAM application which mirror those in the Form A.

The application is signed with a statement of truth, which can be signed by the solicitor on behalf of the client or signed by the client themselves.

The application is made to the Family Court and submitted with a filing fee.

8.4 Financial disclosure

Form E1 'Financial Statement for a financial remedy (other than a financial order or financial relief after an overseas divorce or dissolution etc) in the family court or High Court' is available online at **formfinder.hmctsformfinder.justice.gov.uk/form-e1-eng.pdf.**

The practitioner should note that sometimes the parties agree to use the Form E even though it is not specifically designed to be used in a Children Act 1989 Schedule 1 application.

When the timetable from the court is received after the Form A1 is issued, it usually indicates that the parties should complete the financial statement that they believe is best suited for the proceedings. There is therefore some degree of discretion on the part of the practitioner.

The financial statement in the Form E1 is shorter than the Form E but there are many similarities. For example, the first page contains the same warnings and if parties do not give full frank and clear disclosure of their financial and other circumstances then there are likely to be consequences. An application to set aside any order based upon inadequate disclosure may be one of those consequences.

Section 1 requires the applicant to insert personal information about themselves, their residence and details of all children and dependants involved.

Section 1.9 requires the applicant to give details about their own state of health and that of the children if the applicant thinks this should be taken into account. It is good practice to give full information and attach any relevant documentation. The court will direct expert medical evidence if this is necessary, for example, in circumstances where a child has additional financial requirements as a result of disability. It should be noted, as these matters are dealt with under the Children Act 1989, that FPR 2010 and that Part 25 apply but Practice Direction 25C is more relevant in these proceedings than Practice Direction 25B.

This part broadly follows the outline of the Form E as detailed in **Chapter 3**.

8.5 Employment

Section 2.1 requires the applicant to indicate if they are employed, self-employed, unemployed or a pensioner. They are then directed to a different section of the financial statement to give further details.

SCHEDULE 1 CHILDREN ACT PROCEEDINGS   151

Section 2.2 requires the applicant to complete details of income from employment and mirrors the requirements in the Form E. See commentary in **Chapter 3** for further details.

Section 2.3 requires the applicant to complete details of income from self-employment or partnership and mirrors the requirements in the Form E. See commentary in **Chapter 3** for further details.

Section 3.1 requires details of income from investments; section 3.2 requires details of state benefits; and section 3.3 requires the applicant to disclose any income not disclosed in previous sections. These also mirror the requirements in the Form E. See commentary in **Chapter 3** for further details.

8.6 Capital

Section 4.1 requires information to be provided with regard to any interest in property, land or buildings. This mirrors the requirements in the Form E. See commentary in **Chapter 3** for further details.

Sections 4.2 and 4.3 require information about bank accounts and investments. These sections mirror the requirements in the Form E. See commentary in **Chapter 3** for further details.

Section 4.4 requires information in relation to life policies and endowment policies. This mirrors the requirements in the Form E. See commentary in **Chapter 3** for further details.

Section 4.5 requires details of other assets that have been listed. This mirrors the requirements in the Form E. See commentary in **Chapter 3** for further details.

Section 4.6 requires the applicant to outline any liabilities. This mirrors the requirements in the Form E. See commentary in **Chapter 3** for further details.

8.7 Income needs

The applicant is required to list their regular expenses and although this section of the Form E1 is different from Form E, it is sensible to use a template schedule of outgoings such as that in **Annex 3D** rather than complete the form at section 5.1. Section 5.2 requires information about the needs of the child; this is incorporated at **Annex 3D** and further commentary can be found in **Chapter 3**.

8.8 Financial resources of the children

This provision is not in the Form E and is specific to an application under Schedule 1 to the Children Act 1989. The court can take into account the financial resources of the children and will do so where appropriate. If the parties agree to use the Form E to disclose their resources, the children's finances should be clearly set out.

The form needs to be signed with the statement of truth and the relevant documents need to be attached with a list of documents. An example can be found at **Annex 3B**.

8.9 Final order

The document at **Annex 8B** is the final order in an application under Schedule 1 to the Children Act 1989.

The order is in a familiar format as it uses the standard order precedents referred to in **Chapter 7**. The document starts off with definitions for the parties, the children, the home and the family car.

In the recitals section it is noted that the terms of the order are intended to be in full and final satisfaction of all claims in England and Wales or in any jurisdiction.

The applicant acknowledges that if the respondent dies before her, she will limit any claim against his estate to the loss of periodical payments that she was due to receive.

The respondent gives an undertaking to purchase a new home up to the value of £750,000 and to bear the associated costs. He agrees to grant an irrevocable licence to allow the applicant and children to occupy the property rent-free to the exclusion of the respondent.

The property will be available for the applicant's occupation until one of the trigger events that are set out at para.10 (b)(i)–(v) occurs. These are similar to those found in matrimonial proceedings. The difference is that the home will need to be vacated by the applicant and the children at some point in the future as there will not be an outright transfer in these proceedings. The paragraph is complex as it needs to take into account responsibility for internal decorative repair and external structural repair.

8.10 Orders

Paragraph 11 provides a lump sum order for the sum of £50,000 to be paid to the applicant to assist with moving costs and to furnish the new property.

Paragraph 12 provides for the transfer of the car to the applicant.

Paragraph 13 indicates that the court has jurisdiction to make a maintenance order as the CMS has made a maximum assessment. Payments are to be made at the rate of £30,000 per annum per child until the first occurring of the events listed at 13(b)(i)–(ii).

Paragraph 14 gives the parties permission to produce the order to the CMS if necessary.

Paragraph 15 dismisses the applicant's claims. It should be noted that there is no mutual dismissal of claims as the respondent is the payer.

Paragraph 16 provides for the respondent to pay a fixed sum towards the applicant's costs.

8.11 Conclusion

Applications under Schedule 1 to the Children Act 1989 are very different from applications for a financial order under the Matrimonial Causes Act 1973 or the Civil Partnership Act 2004. The practitioner should be careful not to dabble in these proceedings without first having a clear understanding of the jurisdictional issues and the limited orders that the court will make in these proceedings.

Annex 8A

First letter to applicant in Schedule 1 Children Act claim

Dear [*name of client*]

Thank you for coming to see me with regard to the breakdown of your relationship. As you have [a child/children] together you can make financial applications against [*name of other parent*] for the child(ren)'s benefit.

[I have written to you separately about using non-court dispute resolution. If you and [*name of other parent*] have decided to go to mediation, use collaborative law or arbitration, then you do not need to make financial claims at Court straight away. Hopefully, you will be able to come to an agreement about your financial matters. If that is the case you will not need to make an application for the Court to resolve matters.]

It would be sensible, however, to turn the agreement into a draft consent order which is sent to the Court to confirm the terms of settlement.

You can make the following claims against [*name of other parent*] in respect of [*name(s) of child(ren)*].

Property claims

It is possible for you to make a claim for the Court to transfer or settle property on you or [*name(s) of child(ren)*]. The Court will make this order if it is for the benefit of [*name(s) of child(ren)*].

You should be aware that the Court will only order property to be available while [*name(s) of child(ren)*] [is/are] under the age of 18. Occasionally the Court will extend that period until [*name(s) of child(ren)*] have finished full-time tertiary education. This is usually when the children finish their first degree.

The Court will not make an order to transfer a property to [*name(s) of child(ren)*] outright, the property will always revert back to [*name of other parent*].

Capital orders

The Court can make lump sum orders for expenses that relate to [*name(s) of child(ren)*]. This could be an order for a one-off payment or an order for a series of payments over a period of time. The structure of the payment will depend on the circumstances of the case.

Income orders

The Court may have the power to make income orders for the benefit of the child(ren) of the family.

A. [You will first need to make an application to the Child Maintenance Service to get a maintenance assessment. Please do this as soon as possible.
   If the Child Maintenance Service assesses [*name of other parent*] to pay the maximum sum, the Court will then have the ability to assess additional maintenance for [*name(s) of child(ren)*].]

OR

B. [As [*name*] lives in [a country outside England and Wales] the Court is able to make a maintenance order.]

OR

C. [As [*name(s) of child(ren)*] [is/are] in fee-paying schools, the Court can order [*name of other parent*] to pay these educational expenses.]

OR

D. [As [*name(s) of child(ren)*] [is/are] disabled the Court can order [*name of other parent*] to pay any expenses related to the disability.]

OR

E. [As [*name of step-parent*] is a step-parent [he/she] can be made to pay maintenance by the Court rather than via the Child Maintenance Service.

Payments can be made to you for [*name(s) of child(ren)*]'s benefit or to them directly. These payments should be for [*name(s) of child(ren)*]'s benefit although this can include some of your expenses as their primary carer.

An order will usually be made until the [child(ren)] reach[es] the age of 17. Sometimes the Court will extend these payments beyond [*name(s) of child(ren)*]'s 18th birthday.

Financial support now

The Court can make an order for [*name of other parent*] to pay maintenance for [*name of child(ren)*].

An interim order can include any claim for your legal costs to make the application.

Costs orders

It is possible to get a costs order in these proceedings, but this will be a matter for the Judge to decide. We will ensure that we advise you on these matters if litigation starts.

I hope you understand the orders that the Court is able to make. If you have any questions or queries please do not hesitate to contact me.

Yours sincerely

Annex 8B
Draft order Schedule 1

IN THE FAMILY COURT AT [*location*]

CASE No:

The Children Act 1989

The Child Support Act 1991

The relationship of [*name*] and [*name*]

After hearing [*name the advocate(s) who appeared*]

After consideration of the documents lodged by the parties

ORDER MADE BY [*NAME OF JUDGE*] ON [*DATE*] SITTING IN PRIVATE FOLLOWING A RESERVED JUDGMENT GIVEN ON [*DATE*]

> **WARNING: IF YOU DO NOT COMPLY WITH THIS ORDER, YOU MAY BE HELD TO BE IN CONTEMPT OF COURT AND YOU MAY BE SENT TO PRISON, BE FINED, OR HAVE YOUR ASSETS SEIZED.**

The parties

1. The applicant is [*name of applicant*]

    The respondent is [*name of respondent*]

Definitions

2. Children of the Family

    a.   The 'children of the family' are:

    i.   [*insert details of children in family*]

3. New Home

    a.   The 'new home' shall mean the property agreed between the parties or in default of agreement determined by the court.

4. 'The net proceeds of sale' shall mean the actual sale price of the property concerned (including any sum paid for fixtures and fittings) less the amount outstanding on the mortgage, the solicitors' conveyancing costs, estate agents' costs and any other costs in connection with the sale which have been agreed by the parties.

5. 'The family car' shall mean the [*make and model of car*] vehicle with registration number [*registration number*], currently used by the [applicant]/[respondent].
6. 'CMS' shall mean the Child Support Agency, the Child Maintenance Enforcement Commission, the Child Maintenance Service or such other state appointed agency operating within the United Kingdom as may from time to time replace any of them.
7. 'CMS calculation' shall mean the assessment or calculation or periodic demand by the CMS.

Recitals

8. The parties agree that the terms set out in this order are intended to be in full and final satisfaction of all claims for capital, that is payments of lump sums, transfers of property, and settlements of property that the applicant may have for the benefit of the child[ren] of the family and the child[ren] themselves may have against the respondent under Schedule 1 to the Children Act 1989 or howsoever else arising either in England and Wales or any other jurisdiction.

General Agreements/Declarations

9. The applicant acknowledges that, if the respondent predeceases her, any claim that she may make against the respondent's estate under the Inheritance (Provision for Family and Dependants) Act 1975 shall be limited to seeking a sum to compensate her for the loss of the periodical payments the respondent was ordered to pay her at paragraph [*number*] below for the benefit of the children of the family.

Undertakings to the court

You may be held to be in contempt of court and imprisoned or fined, or your assets may be seized, if you break the promises that you have given to the court.

If you fail to pay any sum of money which you have promised the court that you will pay, a person entitled to enforce the undertaking may apply to the court for an order. You may be sent to prison if it is proved that you –

a) have, or have had since the date of your undertaking, the means to pay the sum; and
b) have refused or neglected, or are refusing or neglecting, to pay that sum.

I understand the undertakings that I have given, and that if I break any of my promises to the court I may be sent to prison for contempt of court.

....

[name]

....

[name]

10.

   a.   The respondent shall purchase the new home up to the value of £750,000. The costs of the purchase shall be borne by the respondent and the conveyancing work in respect of the purchase shall be carried out by a solicitor chosen by the respondent.

   b.   Simultaneously with the purchase of the new home, the respondent shall grant the applicant an irrevocable licence, allowing the applicant and the children of the family to occupy it rent-free to the exclusion of the respondent until the first to happen of the following events ('the determining event'):

       i.   the youngest surviving of the children of the family attaining the age of 18 years or ceasing their full-time tertiary education to first degree level including a gap year, or permanently ceasing to live with the applicant, whichever is the later;

      ii.   the death of the last surviving of the children of the family;

      iii.   the death of the applicant;

      iv.   the applicant's remarriage or cohabitation with another person as man and wife for a continuous period of more than 6 months;

      v.   further order of the court.

   c.   The terms of the irrevocable licence shall be agreed between the parties or in default of agreement determined by the court. The respondent shall be responsible for the costs of preparing and executing agreement in respect of the irrevocable licence.

   d.   The applicant and the children of the family shall occupy the new home under the terms of the irrevocable licence agreement as licensees and shall not, save as provided for in this order, acquire any legal or beneficial interest in it or rights over it.

   e.   The applicant shall discharge as and when each payment becomes due, be solely responsible for and in any event indemnify the respondent against all reasonable sums due in respect of service charge, council tax, utilities (including but not limited to gas, electricity, water and telephone accounts), and buildings and contents insurance premiums in respect of the new home until the applicant and the children of the family vacate the new home.

   f.   The applicant shall be responsible for all routine maintenance and decorative repairs to the property.

   g.   The cost of insuring the property and of carrying out structural repairs [insert definition] shall be the responsibility of the respondent, provided that no works of structural repair shall be carried out to the property unless agreed by the parties or ordered by the court.

   h.   Any works carried out at the new home shall be regulated by the irrevocable licence. If the applicant wishes to spend money on the property to improve its amenities then the parties shall enter into a deed recording the interest (if any) that she will acquire in the net proceeds of sale of the new home in consequence, prior to the commencing of such works. The applicant shall acquire such share in the net proceeds of the new home as may be agreed between the parties or in default of agreement as shall be determined by the court as reflecting the likely increase in the sale price (when the new home is eventually sold) referable to her outlay. The parties shall be equally responsible for the costs of preparing and executing the deed of trust.

i.   If the applicant shall remain in occupation of the property for more than 6 months after the determining event, she shall pay to the respondent from that date such sum by way of occupation rent as may be agreed or in default of agreement determined by the court.

j.   On or before the determining event the applicant shall have the right to purchase the respondent's interest in the property at an open market valuation to be agreed, or in default of agreement to be determined by the court.

Orders

IT IS ORDERED (BY CONSENT)

11. The respondent shall pay to the applicant for the benefit of the children of the family a lump sum of £50,000 42 days after the date of this order to meet the applicant's removal costs and costs of furnishing the children of the family's new home.

12. The respondent shall transfer to the applicant all his interest in the family car for her use for the benefit of the children of the family within 42 days of the date of this order. The applicant shall be responsible for the costs of running and maintaining the family car.

13.

a.   In circumstances where (a) the CMS has made a CMS calculation in respect of the children of the family; and (b) the court is satisfied that the circumstances of the case make it appropriate for the respondent to make periodical payments as ordered in paragraph [*number*] below in addition to the child maintenance payable in accordance with the CMS calculation, the respondent shall pay to the applicant periodical payments for the benefit of the children of the family.

b.   Payments shall be at the rate of £30,000 per annum per child payable monthly in arrears by standing order. Payments shall start on [*date*], and shall end on:

    i.   each child respectively attaining the age of 18 years or ceasing their full-time tertiary education to first degree level including a gap year, or permanently ceasing to live with the applicant, whichever shall be the later; or

    ii.   a further order.

    The court may (prior to the expiry of the term or subsequently) order a longer period of payment.

14. There be permission under FPR 2010, rule 12.73(1)(b) to produce a copy of this order to the CMS.

15. Except as provided for in this order, the applicant's claims for lump sum orders, transfer of property orders, and settlement of property orders for the benefit of the children of the family shall be dismissed, and the applicant shall not be entitled to make a further application for housing provision for the benefit of the children of the family.
16. The respondent shall pay £100,000 towards the applicant's costs by [*date*].
17. The parties shall have liberty to apply to the court concerning the implementation and timing of the terms of this order only.

....

[name]   [name]

Dated: